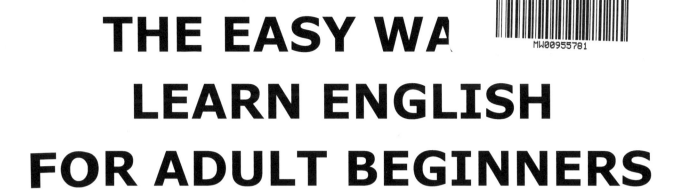

THE EASY WA
LEARN ENGLISH
FOR ADULT BEGINNERS

4 IN 1 BIBLE

Essential English Grammar, Verbs, Common Phrases for Everyday Use, and Workbook to Speak English in No Time

Katrina Beltran

EXTRA BONUS

FLASHCARDS

+

DICTIONARY

TABLE OF CONTENTS

BOOK DESCRIPTION

Embark on a transformative language journey with our comprehensive 4-in-1 collection, designed specifically for adult beginners grappling with the complexities of learning English. Bid farewell to overwhelming grammar rules, frustrating verb conjugations, and the struggle to find practical phrases for everyday conversations. No more aimless learning—this collection provides structured practice for speaking English effortlessly, saving you precious time with its streamlined and effective methods.

What you will Learn Inside the book:

Overwhelmed by Complex Grammar Rules

Simplify your language learning experience by ditching intricate and confusing grammar rules that often leave beginners bewildered.

Difficulty in Memorizing Verbs and Their Conjugations

Say goodbye to the frustration of verb memorization. Our collection offers a simplified approach, making verbs and their conjugations a breeze to master.

Lack of Everyday Phrases for Practical Use

Tired of formal language that doesn't apply to real-life situations? Discover a treasure trove of common phrases designed for everyday use, ensuring you're ready for any conversation.

Absence of Structured Practice for Speaking English

Break free from haphazard learning methods. This collection provides a well-structured workbook, allowing you to practice and apply your newfound knowledge in a way that resonates with real-world scenarios.

Time-Consuming Learning Methods

Wave goodbye to time-consuming techniques that yield minimal results. Our collection is crafted with efficiency in mind, allowing you to grasp the essentials of English swiftly.

Are you tired of drowning in complex grammar rules? Fed up with the never-ending struggle to memorize verbs and their conjugations? Imagine having a repertoire of everyday phrases at your fingertips, ready to use in any situation. No more stumbling through conversations. Picture a structured and efficient way to practice speaking English without wasting precious time on outdated methods. The frustration ends here.

Why buy this book?

Because you deserve an easy and effective path to mastering English. Say farewell to confusion and hello to confidence in your language skills.

Embark on your English learning journey today. Your simplified language experience awaits!

BOOK 1: ESSENTIAL ENGLISH GRAMMAR FOR ADULT BEGINNERS

CHAPTER 1: Introduction to English Grammar

Have you ever felt the excitement of embarking on a journey into the vast realm of a new language? Learning English as an adult may seem like a daunting task, but fear not! This book, "The Easy Way to Learn English for Adult Beginners," is your companion on this thrilling adventure. Whether you're a complete novice or have some basic knowledge, we're here to make your language-learning experience enjoyable and, most importantly, effective.

Learning a new language as an adult comes with its own set of challenges, but it also brings unique rewards. English, being one of the most widely spoken languages globally, opens doors to countless opportunities in communication, career advancement, and cultural exploration. This book is designed with the understanding that adult learners have distinct needs and preferences, and our goal is to cater to those while ensuring a smooth and engaging learning process.

Through carefully crafted lessons, practical exercises, and real-life examples, we aim to demystify the complexities of the English language and empower you to express yourself confidently in various situations. The approach we take is not only systematic but also tailored to make learning enjoyable, turning what might seem like a chore into a fulfilling and enriching experience.

So, are you ready to unlock the doors to a world of new possibilities through the mastery of English? Let's embark on this journey together, where every page brings you closer to fluency and every lesson is a step towards realizing your language-learning goals. Welcome to "The Easy Way to Learn English for Adult Beginners" – your passport to linguistic success!

The English Alphabet and Basic Phonetics

Welcome to the first step in your journey to learn English! In this section, we will explore the foundation of the English language – the alphabet and basic phonetics. Understanding the sounds and letters is crucial for effective communication.

The English Alphabet:
The English alphabet consists of 26 letters, each with its own unique sound and role in forming words. Familiarizing yourself with these letters is the starting point for mastering English. Let's go through them together:

A B C D E F G H I J K L M N O P Q R S T U V W X Y Z

Take your time to practice pronouncing each letter and recognize its written form. This fundamental skill will serve as the building block for your language learning journey.

Basic Phonetics:

Phonetics is the study of speech sounds, and it plays a vital role in English language learning. To begin, let's focus on some basic phonetic concepts:

Consonants and Vowels:

Consonants are sounds produced by restricting or blocking the airflow. Examples include 'b,' 'c,' and 't.'
Vowels, on the other hand, are open sounds produced without any obstruction. Examples include 'a,' 'e,' and 'i.'

Consonant Sounds:

English has a variety of consonant sounds, such as the hard 'g' in "go" or the soft 'th' in "think." Practice these sounds to enhance your pronunciation.

Vowel Sounds:

Vowel sounds can vary greatly in English. Pay attention to the differences between short and long vowels, like the 'i' in "sit" versus "site."

Diphthongs:

Diphthongs are complex vowel sounds formed by combining two simple vowels. Familiarize yourself with examples like the 'oi' in "coin" or 'ou' in "house."

Practice Tips:

- Listen and Repeat:
Immerse yourself in English sounds by listening to native speakers. Repeat after them to improve your pronunciation.

- Use Phonetic Resources:
Explore online resources and dictionaries that provide phonetic transcriptions to guide your pronunciation.

- Word Association:
Associate sounds with words and phrases. This helps reinforce the correct pronunciation and usage.

As you progress, remember that consistency is key. Developing a strong foundation in the alphabet and basic phonetics will pave the way for more advanced language skills.

Basic Sentence Structure: Subject, Verb, Object

In the vast landscape of the English language, understanding the fundamental structure of sentences is akin to unlocking the door to effective communication.

At its core, a sentence typically consists of three essential components: the subject, the verb, and the object. This structure, commonly known as Subject-Verb-Object (SVO), forms the backbone of English sentences and provides a framework for expressing thoughts and ideas.

Subject:

The subject is the focal point of a sentence. It is the entity that performs the action or is described in the sentence. Subjects can be nouns, pronouns, or noun phrases.

For example:

Noun: The cat sat on the windowsill.

Pronoun: She enjoys reading novels.

Noun Phrase: A talented musician played the piano beautifully.

Identifying the subject is crucial, as it helps determine who or what the sentence is about.

Verb:

The verb is the action or state of being in a sentence. It represents what the subject is doing or the condition it is in. Verbs come in various forms, such as action verbs, linking verbs, and auxiliary verbs.

Here are examples:

Action Verb: The dog barked loudly.

Linking Verb: She is a dedicated teacher.

Auxiliary Verb: They have completed their assignments.

Understanding the verb is essential for grasping the dynamics of the sentence and the actions or states being conveyed.

Object:

The object is the recipient of the action performed by the subject. It completes the meaning of the sentence by answering the question "what" or "whom." Objects can be nouns, pronouns, or noun phrases.

Consider these examples:

Noun: He wrote a letter.

Pronoun: She called him.

Noun Phrase: We planted colorful flowers in the garden.

Recognizing the object helps in comprehending the full picture of the action or interaction within the sentence.

Putting it Together:

To construct a basic sentence, one needs to combine these elements in a logical order. The standard arrangement is Subject-Verb-Object, but variations exist for stylistic purposes or to emphasize certain elements.

Consider the following examples:

The students (subject) read (verb) the novel (object).

She (subject) is (verb) an excellent chef (object).

They (subject) built (verb) a sandcastle (object) on the beach.

Mastering the Subject-Verb-Object structure is a significant stride toward building proficiency in English. As you embark on your language learning journey, pay attention to these foundational elements, and soon you'll find yourself constructing sentences with ease and precision.

CHAPTER 2: Understanding Nouns and Pronouns

Nouns and pronouns are fundamental parts of speech in English and play essential roles in constructing sentences. Let's break down each of them.

Types of Nouns: Proper, Common, Abstract

Understanding the different types of nouns is a fundamental step in mastering the English language. Nouns are words that name people, places, things, or ideas. They play a crucial role in constructing sentences and conveying meaning. Let's delve into the various types of nouns to enhance your grasp of this essential aspect of English grammar.

Common Nouns: These are general names for people, places, things, or ideas. Examples include "teacher," "city," "book," and "happiness." Common nouns are not capitalized unless they begin a sentence.

Proper Nouns: Unlike common nouns, proper nouns refer to specific and unique individuals, places, or things and are always capitalized. Examples include "John," "Paris," "The Mona Lisa," and "Coca-Cola."

Concrete Nouns: These nouns represent tangible, physical entities that you can perceive with your senses. Examples include "tree," "dog," "mountain," and "ice cream."

Abstract Nouns: In contrast to concrete nouns, abstract nouns refer to ideas, concepts, emotions, or qualities that are intangible. Examples include "love," "freedom," "happiness," and "justice."

Countable Nouns: These nouns can be counted and have both singular and plural forms. Examples include "apple" (singular) and "apples" (plural).

Uncountable Nouns: These nouns represent substances, concepts, or qualities that cannot be counted individually. Examples include "water," "information," and "happiness." Uncountable nouns do not have a plural form in the same way countable nouns do.

Collective Nouns: These nouns refer to groups of people, animals, or things as a single entity. Examples include "team," "herd," "family," and "flock."
Possessive Nouns: These nouns indicate ownership or possession. They are formed by adding an apostrophe and "s" ('s) to the noun. Examples include "Jane's car," "the dog's collar," and "the company's success."

Countable and Uncountable Nouns

A countable noun can be used in either the singular or plural form.
Example: One/a tree, two trees. Uncountable nouns cannot be counted with numbers. These are normally substances and concepts.
Example: Some milk

We can't use a *number*, nor *a,* or *an* for uncountable nouns. Instead we can use the following;

- Some
- A bit of
- A lot of
- Much
- A handful
- A pinch
- A teaspoon

Examples of uncountable nouns

- Love
- Music
- Money
- Happiness
- Advice
- Sugar
- Rice
- Water
- Milk
- Juice
- Pasta
- Soup

Applying the rule

- Some music
- A lot of love
- A bit of happiness
- Some soup
- Some pasta
- A little bit of milk
- A bit of advice
- Much money

Understanding the distinctions among these types of nouns will significantly enhance your ability to use them correctly in sentences. Practice identifying and using each type to reinforce your grasp of English grammar.

Pronouns and Their Usage

Understanding pronouns is a crucial step in mastering the English language. Pronouns are words that replace nouns, making sentences clearer and more concise. They allow us to refer to people, places, things, and ideas without constantly repeating the same nouns.

Personal Pronouns

Subject Pronouns:

- I
- You
- He
- She
- It
- We
- They

These pronouns replace nouns as the subjects of sentences. For example:
She is a talented musician.
We are going to the park.

Object Pronouns:

- Me
- You
- Him
- Her
- It
- Us
- Them

Object pronouns replace nouns as the objects of verbs or prepositions. For example:
The teacher praised him for his hard work.
She gave the gift to us.

Possessive Pronouns:

- My/Mine
- Your/Yours
- His
- Her/Hers
- Its
- Our/Ours
- Their/Theirs

Possessive pronouns indicate ownership. For example:

This is my book. Is this one yours?
The cat is chasing its tail.

Demonstrative Pronouns

- This
- That
- These
- Those

Demonstrative pronouns point to specific things. For example:
I like this sweater.
Look at those mountains!

Reflexive Pronouns

- Myself
- Yourself
- Himself
- Herself
- Itself
- Ourselves
- Yourselves
- Themselves

Reflexive pronouns are used when the subject and object of a sentence are the same. For example:
She cut herself while cooking.
We enjoyed ourselves at the party.

Interrogative Pronouns

- Who
- Whom
- Whose
- Which
- What

Interrogative pronouns are used to ask questions. For example:

Who is coming to the party?

Which book do you want to read?

Indefinite Pronouns

- All
- Another
- Any
- Anyone
- Anything
- Each
- Either
- Everybody
- Everything
- Neither
- Nobody
- None
- No one
- Nothing
- One
- Other
- Somebody
- Someone
- Something
- Both
- Few
- Many
- Several
- All
- Any
- More
- Most
- None
- Some

Indefinite pronouns refer to nonspecific people, places, or things. For example:

Everybody enjoyed the concert.

Some students are absent today.

Pronouns serve as substitutes to prevent the repetitive use of nouns. While native English speakers may not frequently encounter pronoun errors, it's undeniable that pronouns are a critical element of speech for clear and effective communication, often misapplied by students and other learners.

Mistakes with pronouns typically arise in English when there's a mismatch in number between the pronouns and their corresponding nouns. A singular noun requires a singular pronoun and the same applies for plural forms. Additionally, pronoun errors can stem from a lack of agreement between the verb and the sentence's subject. Notably, these two types of errors are interconnected. Highlighted below are some prevalent pronoun mistakes in grammar. The phrases "one of," "some of," and "none of" should be constructed such that the verb corresponds correctly with the subject. In the examples below, the singular verbs "eats" and "was" correctly align with singular subjects.

Incorrect: One of my classmates eat a lot.

Correct: One of my classmates eats a lot.

Incorrect: Some of the king's servant is here. Correct: Some of the king's servants are here.

Incorrect: None of the athlete were around. Correct: None of the athletes was around.

Incorrect: Each boy and each girl were given an exercise book. Correct: Each boy and each girl was given an exercise book.

It's important to maintain consistency when the word "one" is employed in a sentence; it should be used consistently throughout.

CHAPTER 3: Exploring English Verbs

In short, **verbs** are the doing words. They describe the action. The two types of verbs in English are active and stative. **Active verbs** describe action and movement, like *work*, *study*, *type*, and *walk*. The action can even be a rather inactive one, like *sleep*, *sit*, and *relax*. **Stative verbs** describe a state or condition, like *love*, *feel*, *agree*, and *suppose*.

Active verbs can be used in the progressive form when we indicate actions and movement happening now.

1. Jeff is **working** on the meeting report.
2. The professor is **writing** on the board.
3. I can't chat now. I'm **studying** for the psychology final.

Stative verbs are typically not used in the progressive form when we indicate a state or condition existing now.

1. Tasha **loves** this pizza.
2. That **smells** amazing. What are you cooking?
3. I **agree** with your idea, but I think we should ask the manager first.

Some verbs can be used in both an active and stative way, but when they are used in a progressive form, the meaning is slightly different.

Feel refers to how our senses react to the environment or our body condition.
I **feel** great because I just landed a new job.
Feel is also a special stative verb because we can use it in the progressive with the same meaning.
I'm **feeling** great because I just landed a new job.
On the other hand, **feeling** is similar to **touching** and refers to trying to make physical contact with something.
I'm **feeling** the edge of this cup to check if there are any cracks or chips.
Smell refers to noticing an aroma or odor.
I **smell** pizza. Who brought the pizza into the office? Can I have some?
Smelling refers to using our nose to check the aroma of something.
Sophia: What are you doing?
Liam: I'm **smelling** this pizza to make sure it's not too garlicky. It **smells** good.
Taste refers to the reaction of our tongue to something we put in our mouth.
This alligator **tastes** like chicken.
Tasting refers to using your tongue to sample the flavor of something.

Olivia: What are you doing?

Jackson: I'm *tasting* the soup. I think it needs more salt.

Regular and Irregular Verbs

Regular Verbs

In English, verbs play a crucial role in expressing actions, events, or states. Understanding regular verbs is a fundamental step in mastering the language. Unlike irregular verbs, regular verbs follow a consistent pattern when conjugated in different tenses. This makes them more straightforward for beginners to grasp. Regular verbs are those that form their past tense and past participle by adding "-ed" to the base form of the verb. This rule applies across the board for regular verbs, making it easier to predict their conjugation patterns.

Examples of Regular Verbs:

Walk

Present: I walk to the store every day.

Past: Yesterday, I walked to the store.

Past Participle: I have walked to the store many times.

Play

Present: The children play in the park.

Past: Yesterday, they played in the park.

Past Participle: They have played there before.

Talk

Present: I talk to my friend on the phone.

Past: Last night, I talked to my friend.

Past Participle: I have talked to her many times.

Regular Verb Tenses

Regular verbs maintain a consistent pattern when changing tenses. Here are the basic forms:

Present Tense: The base form of the verb is used in the present tense.
Example: I swim in the pool.

Past Tense: "-ed" is added to the base form for regular verbs in the past tense.
Example: I swam in the pool yesterday.

Past Participle: The past participle is formed by adding "-ed" to the base form and is used with auxiliary verbs like "have" or "has."
Example: I have swum in the pool many times.

Understanding and practicing regular verbs will enhance your ability to communicate effectively in English. Regular verbs are a solid foundation upon which you can build your language skills. Take the time to practice and reinforce these concepts as you progress in your English learning journey.

Irregular Verbs

Understanding irregular verbs is a key aspect of mastering English grammar. Unlike regular verbs that follow a predictable pattern when conjugated, irregular verbs have unique forms for different tenses. While this might seem daunting at first, don't worry – with practice, you'll become more comfortable using irregular verbs in everyday conversation.

Irregular verbs do not conform to the regular pattern of adding "-ed" to form past tense or past participle. Instead, they undergo distinct changes in their base, past tense, and past participle forms. Learning these irregularities is crucial for effective communication in English.

Common Irregular Verbs

Let's explore some frequently used irregular verbs along with their base form, past tense, and past participle:

Go
Base Form: Go
Past Tense: Went
Past Participle: Gone

Take
Base Form: Take
Past Tense: Took
Past Participle: Taken

See
Base Form: See
Past Tense: Saw
Past Participle: Seen

Eat
Base Form: Eat
Past Tense: Ate
Past Participle: Eaten

Have
Base Form: Have
Past Tense: Had
Past Participle: Had

Using Irregular Verbs in Sentences

To apply irregular verbs effectively, it's important to understand how they function in different tenses. Let's consider examples:

Present Tense: "I go to the store every day."
Past Tense: "Yesterday, I went to the store."
Present Perfect: "I have gone to the store multiple times this week."
By incorporating irregular verbs into your daily language practice, you'll build confidence in using them naturally.

Learning irregular verbs is a process that involves consistent practice. Create flashcards, use online resources, and engage in conversations to reinforce your understanding. The more you immerse yourself in the language, the easier it becomes to remember these irregular verb forms.

In conclusion, while irregular verbs may present a challenge, they are an essential part of English grammar. Embrace the learning process, practice regularly, and soon you'll find yourself using irregular verbs effortlessly in your English communication.

Auxiliary Verbs: "Be," "Do," "Have"

Understanding auxiliary verbs is a crucial step in mastering the English language. These verbs, also known as helping verbs, play a significant role in forming tenses, asking questions, and creating negations. The three primary auxiliary verbs in English are "be," "do," and "have."

1. "Be"

The verb "be" is fundamental in English as it is used to form continuous tenses, passive voice, and to indicate states of being. It takes different forms based on the subject and tense of the sentence:

Present Simple: I am, you are, he/she/it is, we/you/they are
Past Simple: I was, you were, he/she/it was, we/you/they were
Present Continuous: I am being, you are being, he/she/it is being, we/you/they are being
Past Continuous: I was being, you were being, he/she/it was being, we/you/they were being

Understanding when to use these forms is essential for constructing clear and accurate sentences.

Rule 1: The "be" verb functions differently than all other verbs in English. It must be changed into [am, is, are] depending on the Subject (I, you, he, she, it, they, we, etc.)

Subject	Be verb (present tense)
I	am
You	are
He	is
She	is
It	is

They	are
We	are

Rule 2: To construct a negative with the "be" verb, use "not" after the verb (am, is, are)

Examples:

- I am **not** at home.
- She is **not** at the park.

- They are **not** happy.

Rule 3: To make a Yes/No question with the "be" verb, use the format:
[be + subject + complement]
Examples:

Be Verb (Is/ Am/ Are)	Subject	Complement
Are	you	at home?
Is	Mr. Smith	sick today?
Am	I	late?

Common Mistake: **I'm late?**

First of all, never use a contraction (I'm) in a question. This may be fine in spoken English if you are simply repeating what someone said to confirm what has been said. However, in written English, the questions with the '*be*' verb need to be in the form of a question: *Am I late?* (the subject **I** must come after the verb **am**).

Rule 4: To make an Information question (Who, What, Where, When, Why, etc.) with the "be" verb, use the following format.
[Wh word + be verb + subject + complement]
Remember that the subject decides which form of the be verb (am, is, are)
Examples:

Wh word	(is/ am/ are)	Subject	(complement)
Where	are	you	from?
Why	are	we	here?
Who	is	that girl?	
When	is	your appointment?	
What	am	I	for Halloween?
How	are	you?	

Other Things to Note: Contractions

In spoken English especially, contractions are used. Contractions are fine in written English as well, but if you are writing a formal essay, letter, or any other formal type of writing, avoid using them. Use the following table as a reference.

Formal	Contraction (affirmative)	Contraction (negative)
I am	I'm	I'm not
You are	You're	You're not/ You aren't
He is	He's	He's not/ He isn't
She is	She's	She's not/ She isn't
They are	They're	They're not/ They aren't
We are	We're	We're not/ We aren't
It is	It's	It's not/ It isn't

2. "Do"

The verb "do" is commonly used as an auxiliary verb in questions, negatives, and emphatic statements. It is also used in the formation of the present simple tense for most verbs:

- Present Simple: I/you/we/they do, he/she/it does
- Past Simple: I/you/he/she/it/we/they did

Additionally, "do" is used to create emphasis, especially in affirmative sentences: "I do enjoy learning English."

3. "Have"

The verb "have" is used as an auxiliary verb in perfect tenses, indicating actions that are completed or ongoing up to a certain point in the past, present, or future:

- Present Perfect: I/you/we/they have + past participle, he/she/it has + past participle
- Past Perfect: I/you/he/she/it/we/they had + past participle
- Future Perfect: I/you/he/she/it/we/they will have + past participle
- Understanding the use of "have" in these contexts is essential for conveying the timing and completion of actions.

Mastering these three auxiliary verbs, "be," "do," and "have," lays a solid foundation for constructing a variety of sentences in English. Practice using them in different contexts to enhance your language skills and communicate effectively.

CHAPTER 4: Mastering Tenses in English

Navigating through English tenses is crucial for crafting clear and impactful communication. Every tense in the English language plays a unique role in pinpointing the timing of actions or states. This chapter provides a comprehensive guide to the fundamental tenses, offering insights and strategies for their adept utilization.

The acquisition of proper tense usage is indispensable for articulate communication in English. Tenses function as markers, signaling the temporal aspect of actions or states, thus enabling precise and coherent expression. We'll explore the essential English tenses, offering guidelines and strategies to facilitate their seamless integration into your linguistic skill set.

Present Tense

The journey through English tenses introduces us to a spectrum of complexity, from the straightforward to the intricate. Though it would be ideal to have a single, uniform structure, the reality is a bit more complex. However, this guide aims to simplify each category, enhancing your understanding and application.

Simple Present Tense

Consider this sentence: "I am happy to learn grammar, as I write every day." This epitomizes the simple present tense, typically used to portray current actions or habitual activities. It encapsulates ongoing states like my happiness in learning grammar or recurring actions, exemplified by my daily writing habit.

Conjugating the simple present tense is generally straightforward. Most verbs adopt their base form or append an 's' or 'es' for different pronouns, except for the verb 'to be,' which follows its unique pattern.

Below is a table demonstrating the simple present tense conjugation:

Pronoun	Verb 'To Write'	Verb 'To Be'
First-person singular	I write	I am
Second-person singular	You write	You are
Third-person singular	He/She/It writes	He/She/It is
First-person plural	We write	We are
Second-person plural	You write	You are
Third-person plural	They write	They are

To formulate negative statements in the simple present tense, introduce 'do not' (or 'don't') before the verb. For instance, "I do not want to go to the park." However, for the verb 'to be,' insert 'not' after the verb, as in "I am not happy."

Using the simple present tense for experiences or general truths can be illustrated with sentences like "I have traveled to China before," indicating a past experience that is relevant to the present.

Grasping the nuances of the present tense paves the way for clear and effective communication. As we progress, we'll explore more tenses, each with its distinct function and form, to enrich your understanding and mastery of English.

Present Perfect Tense

The present perfect tense offers a unique perspective on time, depicting events that occurred in the past without specifying the exact moment or illustrating actions that started in the past and persist to the present moment. For instance, using the term 'have' followed by a past participle verb indicates a past action with an unspecified timeline, as in having traveled to China at an undefined point in the past.

Conjugating the present perfect tense involves the simple addition of 'have' or 'has' prior to the past participle of a verb:

Pronoun	Conjugation
First-person singular	I have traveled
Second-person singular	You have traveled
Third-person singular	He/She/It has traveled
First-person plural	We have traveled
Second-person plural	You have traveled
Third-person plural	They have traveled

To form negative sentences in the present perfect tense, insert 'not' immediately after 'have' or 'has', as in "I have not traveled to China before."

Present Continuous Tense

The present continuous tense is adept at capturing actions unfolding at the current moment or imminent future, such as a taxi actively waiting outside.

To form the present continuous tense, combine the present tense of the verb 'to be' with the present participle (ending in 'ing') of the main verb, thereby indicating ongoing or imminent actions.

The conjugation pattern for the present continuous tense is as follows:

Pronoun	Conjugation
First-person singular	I am waiting
Second-person singular	You are waiting
Third-person singular	He/She/It is waiting

Pronoun	Conjugation
First-person plural	We are waiting
Second-person plural	You are waiting
Third-person plural	They are waiting

To express negation in the present continuous tense, add 'not' following the verb 'to be', as in "I am not waiting any longer."

Past Tense

Navigating through the past tense involves recounting actions that have already occurred. While it might seem straightforward, it's easy to mistakenly intertwine past tense verbs with present tense ones within sentences. To maintain clarity and consistency, it's crucial to scrutinize your sentences, ensuring that verbs are accurately conjugated in the past tense.

Simple Past Tense

Consider this statement: "I learned a lot from my English professor." This exemplifies the simple past tense, utilized to denote actions that transpired in the past.

Conjugating the simple past tense for regular verbs is a breeze: typically, you append 'ed' to the root form of the verb:

Pronoun	Conjugation
First-person singular	I learned
Second-person singular	You learned
Third-person singular	He/She/It learned
First-person plural	We learned
Second-person plural	You learned
Third-person plural	They learned

However, when dealing with irregular verbs, the path becomes less straightforward. For many irregular verbs, memorization is key. Here's a classic example:

Pronoun	Conjugation
First-person singular	I was
Second-person singular	You were
Third-person singular	He/She/It was
First-person plural	We were

Pronoun	Conjugation
Second-person plural	You were
Third-person plural	They were

Constructing negative sentences in the simple past also demands special attention. For most verbs, integrate 'did not' before the base form of the verb, as in: "That is strange, I did not learn anything from that professor." This structure can be misleading as it resembles the present tense.

For the verb 'to be,' transition to the negative by adding 'was not' or 'were not' after the verb: "I was not happy."

Mastering the simple past tense and its nuances ensures that your narrative of past events is clear and precise, enhancing the coherence and richness of your communication.

Past Perfect Tense

Consider the situation: "I was shocked to discover that my dog had eaten the entire birthday cake." This scenario illustrates the past perfect tense, a nuanced tense used to narrate a sequence of events that happened in the past. It's less prevalent than the simple past tense, which sometimes leads to its misuse or misunderstanding. Simply put, the past perfect tense is ideal for detailing events that occurred sequentially in the past.

In the given example, the initial shock (expressed in the simple past tense) sets the stage for revealing the reason behind it: the dog's unexpected feast on the birthday cake, depicted using the past perfect tense ('had eaten'). This sequence of events – the shock followed by the revelation – is a classic utilization of the past perfect tense. Conjugating the past perfect tense is relatively straightforward – just place 'had' before the past participle of the verb:

Pronoun	Conjugation
First-person singular	I had eaten
Second-person singular	You had eaten
Third-person singular	He/She/It had eaten
First-person plural	We had eaten
Second-person plural	You had eaten
Third-person plural	They had eaten

To craft a negative sentence in the past perfect tense, insert 'not' immediately after 'had': "They demanded I leave the restaurant even though I had not eaten yet."

Past Continuous Tense

The past continuous tense, the final past tense variant addressed here, is adept at depicting actions that extended over a period in the past. For instance, "Even though the sun was shining all summer, I could not find happiness in it." This tense captures the prolonged nature of the sun's shine throughout the summer season. It's a tense that's often juxtaposed with the present tense, so understanding its purpose is paramount.

Conjugating the past continuous tense involves combining 'was' or 'were' with the present participle (ending in 'ing'):

Pronoun	Conjugation
First-person singular	I was waiting
Second-person singular	You were waiting
Third-person singular	He/She/It was waiting
First-person plural	We were waiting
Second-person plural	You were waiting
Third-person plural	They were waiting

To form a negative sentence in the past continuous tense, just add 'not' after the verb 'to be': "Don't worry, I was not waiting for too long."

Understanding the nuanced uses of the past perfect and past continuous tenses enriches your storytelling capabilities, allowing you to narrate past events with depth and clarity.

Future Tense

Exploring the future tense unfolds the realm of events yet to occur, the anticipatory moments we eagerly await, or the envisioned outcomes we speculate about.

Whether it's orchestrating upcoming engagements with companions or hypothesizing the outcome of the next big game, the future tense is your linguistic tool for projecting into what lies ahead.

Simple Future Tense

Consider the assertion, "By the end of the year, I will have mastered a new language." This sentence exemplifies the simple future tense, envisioning a scenario where the skill of learning a new language unfolds in times yet to come. Conjugating the simple future tense is a breeze: simply precede the base form of the verb with 'will', or opt for the 'am/is/are going to' structure.

Pronoun	'Will' Construction	'Going to' Construction
First-person singular	I will learn	I am going to learn
Second-person singular	You will learn	You are going to learn
Third-person singular	He/She/It will learn	He/She/It is going to learn
First-person plural	We will learn	We are going to learn
Second-person plural	You will learn	You are going to learn
Third-person plural	They will learn	They are going to learn

While both 'I will learn' and 'I am going to learn' nestle within the simple future tense and share identical meanings, 'will' is typically seen as more formal, whereas 'going to' leans towards a more casual tone.

To formulate a negative sentence in the simple future using 'will', append 'not' right after 'will': "You will not learn anything if you remain distracted during class."
For negative sentences employing 'going to', integrate 'not' preceding the phrase: "I am not going to study French this year, contrary to my New Year's resolution."

Future Perfect Tense

Delve into the sentence, "By the time I arrive, he will have already departed." The future perfect tense may initially seem counterintuitive, as it uses a past participle to talk about future events. Nevertheless, it's the optimal tense for expressing an action set to be completed before another future event. In our example, the future perfect ('will have left') articulates an action (someone leaving) that concludes before another future action (your arrival).
Conjugating the future perfect tense is straightforward: simply pair 'will have' with the past participle of the verb.

Pronoun	Conjugation
First-person singular	I will have left
Second-person singular	You will have left
Third-person singular	He/She/It will have left
First-person plural	We will have left
Second-person plural	You will have left
Third-person plural	They will have left

To express the future perfect tense in the negative form, insert 'not' before 'have': "They hopefully will not have departed by the time we get there."

Navigating through the various forms of the future tense in English empowers you to articulate aspirations, plans, and predictions with precision and clarity, painting a vivid linguistic picture of the times ahead.

Future Continuous Tense:

Imagine announcing with pride that a loved one will participate in a significant event, like "My sister will be running in the marathon this year." This example illustrates the future continuous tense, highlighting the ongoing nature of the action (running) set in a future timeframe (this year).

It's essential to note that the future continuous tense is most appropriately used with verbs depicting continuous, active actions (e.g., running, walking, swimming). Using it with static verbs might lead to awkward or ironic interpretations, so for those verbs, it's safer to revert to the simple future tense.

Conjugation of the Future Continuous Tense:

Conjugating verbs in the future continuous tense involves coupling 'will be' with the present participle form of the verb (ending in '-ing'). This formation beautifully captures the essence of actions unfolding over time in the future.

Here's a conjugation table for the future continuous tense:

Person	Positive Statement	Negative Statement
First-person singular	I will be running	I will not be running
Second-person singular	You will be running	You will not be running
Third-person singular	He/She/It will be running	He/She/It will not be running
First-person plural	We will be running	We will not be running
Second-person plural	You will be running	You will not be running
Third-person plural	They will be running	They will not be running

Formulating negative statements in this tense is straightforward: insert 'not' between 'will' and 'be'. For instance, if an unforeseen circumstance arises, one might say, "Jessica will not be running today."

Navigating the Future Continuous Tense:

While the future continuous tense may seem complex due to its structure, it's a highly effective way to express future actions with a sense of continuity and progression. As you acquaint yourself with this tense, remember it's predominantly used for action verbs that inherently imply a duration.

In your journey to master various tenses, it's prudent to approach the future continuous with awareness and clarity. Scrutinize your habitual use of tenses and consciously practice differentiating them. This may require revisiting examples multiple times, but rest assured, with practice, fluency in the future continuous tense will certainly be within your grasp.

CHAPTER 5: The Role of Adjectives and Adverbs

Adjectives and adverbs are two important parts of speech that play distinct roles in enhancing the quality of communication and providing additional information about nouns (adjectives) and verbs, adjectives, or other adverbs (adverbs). Here's an overview of their roles:

Mastering The Role of Adjectives in English

Adjectives enrich our language by describing or modifying nouns, pronouns, or even other adjectives. They inject vividness and specificity, enabling speakers and writers to craft more impactful, detailed narratives. Adjectives can portray a wide array of characteristics, encompassing aspects like size, color, shape, emotions, and opinions.

The primary function of adjectives is to furnish additional insights about a noun or pronoun. They address queries such as "What kind?" "Which one?" or "How many?" Integrating adjectives in sentences allows for the creation of richer, more vivid imagery for the audience.

Grasping the diverse categories of adjectives is crucial for their effective utilization. The main types include:

- Descriptive Adjectives: These provide attributes and qualities of the noun they're associated with. E.g., "The magnificent sunset adorned the sky."
- Quantitative Adjectives: These denote the quantity or number of the noun. E.g., "I possess three novels on the shelf."
- Demonstrative Adjectives: Words like "this," "that," "these," and "those," which indicate the proximity or remoteness of the noun. E.g., "I favor this coat."
- Comparative and Superlative Adjectives: Used for expressing varying degrees of a quality. E.g., "She is taller than her sibling," or "Mount Everest stands as the tallest mountain."

To avoid common pitfalls in adjective usage, consider these guidelines:

- Steer clear of double comparatives. Incorrect: James is more bigger than Joseph. Correct: James is bigger than Joseph.
- 'Many' aligns with countable nouns (e.g., miles, books), whereas 'much' pairs with uncountable nouns (water, air). Similarly, 'less' is for uncountable nouns, and 'fewer' for countable nouns. Incorrect: This race has much miles to traverse. Correct: This race has many miles to traverse.

Incorrect: The stew contains many water. Correct: The stew contains much water.

Incorrect: I hold less queries to address. Correct: I hold fewer queries to address.

- For simple comparisons, append "-er" to adjectives like strong, fat, tall. Incorrect: The lad grew strong and strong. Correct: The lad grew stronger and stronger.
- Position qualifiers like "both," and "all" before possessive terms. Incorrect: He forfeited his all investments. Correct: He forfeited all his investments.
- Use 'farther' for physical distance and 'further' for metaphorical or non-physical distance. Incorrect: Which location is further? Correct: Which location is farther?
- When expressing preference, use 'to' instead of 'from.' Incorrect: I prefer biking from skating. Correct: I prefer biking to skating.
- Position the superlative adjective (e.g., most) towards the end of sentences. Incorrect: My sibling is the most resourceful and skilled individual I've encountered. Correct: My sibling is the most skilled and resourceful individual I've encountered.

Using adjectives before a noun like *car* is the easy way to use an adjective. But we can also use adjectives with the *be* verb and verbs like *feel*, *seem*, *look*, etc.
1. I am **glad** you like your present.
2. I feel **tired**, so I'm going to take a nap.
3. It seems **cold** outside. Please bundle up.

We use adjectives to give more information about nouns and situations. In English, we usually use the adjective *before* the noun.
1. He has a **new** pen.
2. We had a **delicious** pizza.

We tend to use adjectives *after* measurement nouns.
1. The pond in Central Park is about one foot **deep**.
2. My sister is two years **younger** than me.

With *so* and *such,* we use *so* followed by an adjective and *such* followed by a noun phrase, which is a noun preceded by an adjective (like *warm day* and *nice guy*).
1. It's **so** warm today. → It's **such** a warm day.
2. He's **so** nice. → He's **such** a nice guy.

We use *nice and* followed by an adjective to show that something or someone is comfortable or pleasant.
1. Mom's chicken soup will make you feel **nice and** warm.
2. We got to the airport **nice and** early, so we had a drink in the lounge.

Mastering The Role of Adverbs in English

Adverbs, versatile modifiers, enhance the meaning of verbs, adjectives, or other adverbs, answering "how," "when," "where," "why," and "to what extent." Recognizing and skillfully using adverbs is pivotal in language mastery.

Types of Adverbs and Their Functions

Adverbs come in various types, each serving a unique purpose:

- **Adverbs of Manner**: Describe the way an action is performed (e.g., "quickly," "carefully").
- **Adverbs of Frequency**: Indicate the regularity of an action (e.g., "always," "rarely").
- **Adverbs of Time**: Specify the timing of an action (e.g., "yesterday," "soon").
- **Adverbs of Place**: Detail the location of an action (e.g., "here," "everywhere").

Placement and Usage of Adverbs

Understanding the placement of adverbs in a sentence is essential to express your intended meaning accurately. While adverbs typically modify the word they immediately precede, exceptions exist. Mastering these nuances ensures clarity and precision in communication.

Avoiding Overuse and Misplacement

Beware of overusing certain adverbs like "very" and "really." Opt for varied and nuanced adverbs to add richness to your language. Additionally, navigate the intricacies of double negatives and the positioning of adverbs in relation to adjectives to maintain clarity.

Specific Adverb Usage Guidelines

- **Using 'much' in Comparisons**: "Much" is best used in comparisons or with past participles.
- Incorrect: Joe is more taller than his sister.
- Correct: Joe is much taller than his sister.

Employing 'so' and 'too' Correctly:

- Use 'so' with 'that' to indicate a consequence.
- Incorrect: The lion is tough, other animals tremble at its roar.
- Correct: The lion is so tough that other animals tremble at its roar.
- Use 'too' with 'to' to indicate excessiveness.
- Incorrect: The candidate is too good for the job.
- Correct: The candidate is too good to do the job.

Avoiding Double Negatives with Certain Adverbs:
- Incorrect: Lisa barely never comes to class.
- Correct: Lisa barely comes to class.
- Incorrect: I hardly don't know anyone in the church.
- Correct: I hardly know anyone in the church.

Correct Use of 'as' in Descriptions:
- Incorrect: He was described a bully.
- Correct: He was described as a bully.
- Incorrect: Albert Einstein is called as genius.
- Correct: Albert Einstein is called a genius.

Responding to Questions Appropriately:
- Incorrect: Have you eaten today? No, I have eaten.
- Correct: Have you eaten today? No, I have not eaten.

Placement with Intransitive Verbs:
- Incorrect: The lady confidently spoke to the tough guy.
- Correct: The lady spoke confidently to the tough guy.

Embracing the use of adverbs enriches communication, offering nuanced and vivid descriptions. Regularly practicing their use, particularly focusing on their placement and the impact they deliver, is a solid step toward fluency and eloquence.

Comparative and Superlative Forms

Mastering Comparative Adjectives

Comparative adjectives are an essential aspect of English grammar, allowing us to compare and contrast different things, people, or ideas. In this section, we will delve into the nuances of using comparative adjectives effectively, providing you with the tools to express comparisons with confidence.

Comparative adjectives are used to compare two or more things and typically end in "-er" or are preceded by the word "more." For example, "taller," "smarter," and "more interesting" are comparative adjectives. Understanding when to use these forms is crucial for accurate communication.

One-Syllable Adjectives:

For most one-syllable adjectives, you can simply add "-er" to form the comparative. For instance:
- Tall → Taller
- Fast → Faster
- Bright → Brighter

Two-Syllable Adjectives:
When dealing with two-syllable adjectives, it depends on the ending. If the adjective ends in "y," change the "y" to "i" and add "-er." For example:

- Happy → Happier
- Busy → Busier

If the two-syllable adjective does not end in "y," use "more" before the adjective. For example:

- Modern → More modern
- Famous → More famous

Irregular Comparatives:
Some adjectives have irregular comparative forms and do not follow the standard rules. Examples include:

- Good → Better
- Bad → Worse
- Far → Farther (for physical distance) or Further (for metaphorical distance)

Using "Than" in Comparisons:
When making comparisons, the word "than" is often used to connect the two elements being compared. For example:

- She is taller than her brother.
- This book is more interesting than the one I read last month.

Mastering Superlative Adjectives
Understanding superlative adjectives is a crucial step in elevating your English language skills. Superlatives are used to express the highest degree of a quality among three or more things. In this section, we will delve into the nuances of superlative adjectives, providing you with the knowledge and tools needed to use them effectively.

Superlative adjectives are used to compare three or more items in a group, highlighting the one with the highest degree of a particular quality. They are formed by adding the suffix "-est" to the adjective or by using the word "most" before the adjective. For example, "fast" becomes "fastest," and "beautiful" becomes "most beautiful."

Forming Superlatives
a. One-Syllable Adjectives:
For one-syllable adjectives, add "-est" to the adjective.
Example: Fast → Fastest

b. One-Syllable Adjectives ending in 'e':
If the one-syllable adjective ends in 'e,' simply add "-st."

Example: Large → Largest

c. One-Syllable Adjectives ending in a single consonant with a single vowel before it:
Double the final consonant before adding "-est."
Example: Big → Biggest

d. Two-Syllable Adjectives ending in 'y':
Change the 'y' to 'i' and add "-est."
Example: Happy → Happiest

e. Adjectives with Two or More Syllables:
Use "most" before the adjective.
Example: Beautiful → Most beautiful

Some adjectives have irregular forms in the superlative degree. Memorizing these exceptions will enhance your mastery of superlative adjectives. Common irregular superlatives include:

- Good → Best
- Bad → Worst
- Far → Farthest or Furthest

Common Mistakes to Avoid
a. Double Comparisons:
Avoid using both "more" and "-est" together. Choose one form.
Incorrect: He is more tallest than his brother.
Correct: He is taller than his brother.

b. Using Superlatives with Two Items:
Superlatives should involve three or more items. For two items, use the comparative form.
Incorrect: She is the smartest in the class.
Correct: She is smarter than everyone else in the class.

By mastering superlative adjectives, you'll enhance your ability to express comparisons and communicate with precision. Practice these concepts regularly to solidify your understanding and boost your confidence in using superlatives in everyday conversations and writing.

CHAPTER 6: Effective Use of Prepositions

Prepositions, integral elements of English, establish connections between nouns (or pronouns) and other sentence components. Their mastery is pivotal for conveying relationships such as location, time, and direction with clarity and precision.

Prepositions act as linguistic bridges, linking various sentence elements and providing context in terms of time, location, and relation. These typically short words precede nouns or phrases, connecting aspects like time, place, individuals, and objects. Common examples include "of," "to," "under," "in," "into," and "with."
Errors often arise in the three primary preposition categories: time, place, and direction.

Preposition of Time

These prepositions pinpoint the timing of events, whether past, present, or future. Notable examples include "at," "on," "in," "before," and "after."

1. **In**
- **Usage**: For months, years, seasons, and parts of the day.
- **Example**: Born in January; meeting in 2022; vacation in summer; meet in the morning.

2. **On**
- **Usage**: For specific days and dates.
- **Example**: Meeting on Monday; concert on March 15th.

3. **At**
- **Usage**: For specific times and holiday periods.
- **Example**: Train at 3:30 PM; see you at Christmas.

4. **During**
- **Usage**: For the duration or entirety of an event.
- **Example**: Slept during the movie; visited during vacation.

5. **For**
- **Usage**: For the duration of an action or event.
- **Example**: Studying English for two years; staying for a week.

Usage Guidelines for Prepositions of Time
- **On** for days and dates:
- Incorrect: School resumes *in* Monday.

- Correct: School resumes *on* Monday.
- **In** for years, months, seasons, centuries, and times of day:
- Incorrect: Married *on* 2002; vacation *on* spring.
- Correct: Married *in* 2002; vacation *in* spring.
- **At** for precision and exactness:
- Incorrect: Lines meet *in* exactly 90 degrees; dinner *in* 7 p.m.
- Correct: Lines meet *at* exactly 90 degrees; dinner *at* 7 p.m.
- Avoid incorrect usage of other time prepositions:
- Incorrect: Rally *around* the month; sun comes out *around* 6 a.m.
- Correct: Rally *throughout* the month; sun comes out *about* 6 a.m.

Through adept use of prepositions of time, you can precisely articulate temporal concepts, enhancing both spoken and written English. Consistent practice in daily conversations and written communications is instrumental in refining your proficiency.

Ultimately, the key to preposition mastery is regular practice. As you integrate these prepositions into your daily language use, their application in expressing time-related nuances will become increasingly natural and instinctive.

Preposition of Place

Understanding prepositions of place is essential for effective communication in English. These small words, such as in, on, under, above, between, and next to, play a crucial role in describing the location of objects and people. Let's delve into mastering these prepositions to enhance your ability to express positions accurately.

1. In

We use "in" to indicate something is enclosed or surrounded by something else. For example:

- The cat is in the box.
- I live in a small town.

2. On

"On" is used to show that something is physically in contact with a surface. Examples include:

- The book is on the table.
- The picture hangs on the wall.

3. Under

"Under" indicates that one thing is below or beneath another. For instance:

- The keys are under the newspaper.
- The cat is under the bed.

4. Above

"Above" denotes that one thing is higher than another. Consider the following:

- The sun is above the clouds.
- Hang the painting above the sofa.

5. Between

When something is positioned in the middle of two objects or places, we use "between." Examples include:

- The school is between the bank and the supermarket.
- The cat is sitting between the two cushions.

6. Next to

To convey proximity or closeness, we use "next to." For example:

- My house is next to the park.
- The coffee mug is next to the computer.

These are prepositions that indicate position. Avoid the errors shown in the following examples:

Incorrect: There is something hanging *in* the wall.
Correct: There is something hanging *on* the wall.

Incorrect: Maxwell is *at* Dubai, visiting his niece *at* the hospital.
Correct: Maxwell is *in* Dubai, visiting his niece *in* the hospital.

Incorrect: I am *on* the crossroads.
Correct: I am *at* the crossroads.

Incorrect: Let us meet *in* the airport.
Correct: Let us meet *at* the airport.

Use "inside" to indicate nonabstract positions and "in" for abstract positions.

Incorrect: The manual is locked *in* the car.
Correct: The manual is locked *inside* the car.

By practicing these prepositions of place in various contexts, you'll gain confidence in expressing locations accurately. Incorporate them into your everyday conversations and observations, and soon you'll find yourself effortlessly describing where things are in English.

Prepositions of Movement

Understanding how to correctly use prepositions is crucial for effective communication, and it is particularly essential when describing the direction and manner in which people, objects, or animals move.

1. Towards or Away: The Basics of Direction

Prepositions such as "towards" and "away from" are fundamental when describing movement. Whether it's a person walking towards a destination or an object moving away from a point, these prepositions play a vital role in providing clear and concise information.

Example:

The cat walked towards the open door.

She stepped away from the busy street.

2. Into, Onto, and Out of: Precision in Movement

When an action involves transitioning from one place to another, the prepositions "into," "onto," and "out of" become invaluable. They help convey a sense of movement with precision.

Example:

He jumped into the pool with excitement.

The bird flew onto the branch gracefully.

They climbed out of the deep cave cautiously.

3. Along, Across, and Through: Navigating Spaces

Navigating through spaces requires specific prepositions to accurately depict the movement. "Along," "across," and "through" guide the reader or listener to visualize the path taken.

Example:

We strolled along the picturesque beach.

The children ran across the spacious playground.

The hikers trekked through the dense forest.

4. Up, Down, and Around: Vertical and Circular Movements

Describing vertical and circular movements is made seamless with prepositions like "up," "down," and "around." Whether it's climbing stairs or exploring a circular path, these prepositions add depth to the narrative.

Example:

He climbed up the steep mountain.

The elevator descended down to the ground floor.

They walked around the beautiful garden.

5. Over and Under: Crossing Obstacles

Negotiating obstacles is a common scenario in movement. "Over" and "under" provide clarity when describing how someone or something surpasses or passes beneath an obstacle.

Example:

She jumped over the puddle to avoid getting wet.

The agile athlete slid under the bar effortlessly.

6. Towards a Fluent Expression: Practice Exercises

To solidify your understanding of prepositions of movement, engage in various practice exercises. These can involve describing scenes, narrating actions, and creating your own sentences to reinforce the correct usage of prepositions.

Mastering prepositions of movement is an essential step towards achieving fluency in English. By incorporating these prepositions seamlessly into your language skills, you'll enhance your ability to communicate effectively and precisely convey the dynamics of movement in various contexts.

Common Prepositional Phrases

Understanding and using prepositional phrases is a crucial aspect of mastering the English language. Prepositions are words that show the relationship between a noun or pronoun and other elements in a sentence. Learning common prepositional phrases will enhance your ability to express ideas clearly and accurately. Let's delve into some essential prepositional phrases that will aid you in everyday communication.

At the Park:

"I love spending time at the park."

"We'll meet you at the park entrance."

Understanding when to use "at" in relation to specific locations, such as parks, buildings, or specific points, is vital for expressing your whereabouts.

In the Classroom:

"Students learn best when they are actively engaged in activities in the classroom."

"The teacher is always available to help you in the classroom."

Utilizing "in" correctly when referring to an enclosed space or a general location, like a classroom, will help you provide clear descriptions.

On the Weekend:

"I usually relax and catch up on my reading on the weekend."

"Let's plan a movie night on the weekend."
Recognizing when to use "on" for days of the week, including weekends, ensures accurate communication when discussing timeframes.

By the River:
"We found a peaceful spot by the river for a picnic."
"There's a beautiful walking trail by the river."
Employing "by" to denote proximity or location alongside a particular object or area is a valuable skill for expressing spatial relationships.

With a Friend:
"I prefer going to the movies with a friend."
"She celebrated her birthday with friends."
Grasping the use of "with" when indicating accompaniment or association is essential for conveying relationships in your conversations.
For Example:
"Learning prepositional phrases is crucial for effective communication, for example."
"She enjoys various outdoor activities, for example, hiking and biking."

Utilizing "for" in the context of providing examples will help you articulate ideas with clarity and precision.

Remember, mastering prepositional phrases is an ongoing process. Practice incorporating these phrases into your everyday conversations and written expressions to solidify your understanding. As you become more familiar with these common prepositional phrases, you'll find yourself expressing ideas in English with confidence and accuracy.

CHAPTER 7: Conjunctions and Linking Ideas

Conjunctions are linguistic tools that bridge words, sentences, and clauses, adding coherence and structure to communication. For instance, in "He was playing music, yet I studied," the word "yet" connects two distinct sentences, forming a compound statement. Despite their pivotal role, conjunctions are often misapplied. To ensure clarity and correct usage, consider the following guidelines:

Use "not only" in conjunction with "but also":
- Incorrect: She did not only hug him, she kissed him.
- Correct: Not only did she hug him, but she also kissed him.

Prefer "though" over "although" for a lighter nuance:
- Incorrect: You look as although you have seen a monster!
- Correct: You look as though you have seen a monster!

When using "lest," avoid "not" as it already implies negation, and consider following it with "should":
- Incorrect: You had better work hard lest not you become poor.
- Correct: You had better work hard lest you should become poor.

Use "or else" for conditions not covered by "should" or "shall":
- Incorrect: Drive fast to the airport else, you will miss your flight.
- Correct: Drive fast to the airport, or else you will miss your flight.

Pair "both" with "and" for correct linkage:
- Incorrect: Both Jackson, Julian are together.
- Correct: Both Jackson and Julian are together.

Distinguish between "other," "rather," and "than" for accurate comparisons:
- Incorrect: I would leave than sit here with you.
- Correct: I would rather leave than sit here with you.

Understand the difference between "if" (conditional) and "whether" (indicating a choice or uncertainty):
- Incorrect: He doesn't come early, he will not be allowed entry.
- Correct: If he doesn't come early, he will not be allowed entry.

Employ "either...or" and "neither...nor" for clear alternatives or negations:
- Incorrect: We came to the spa but we didn't meet Jane and John.
- Correct: We came to the spa but met neither Jane nor John.

Use "such...that" for emphasizing the extent or consequence:
- Incorrect: The rubber stretched that it broke.
- Correct: The rubber was stretched such that it broke.

Choose "like" for similarities (followed by a noun or pronoun) and "as" for comparisons involving clauses:
- Incorrect: She sang alike as my sister.

- Correct: She sang like my sister.

Avoid redundancy in conjunction use:
- Incorrect: The director asked that what was his grade.
- Correct: The director asked what his grade was.

Use "so as" for indicating purpose:
- Incorrect: He attended the gathering so that he can catch the perpetrators.
- Correct: He attended the gathering so as to catch the perpetrators.

By adhering to these rules, you ensure your sentences are not only grammatically correct but also logically structured, enhancing the clarity and effectiveness of your communication.

Coordinating, Subordinating, and Correlative Conjunctions

Understanding and utilizing coordinating conjunctions is a key aspect of mastering English grammar. Coordinating conjunctions are small but powerful words that connect words, phrases, or clauses of equal importance within a sentence. In this section, we will explore the common coordinating conjunctions and learn how to use them effectively to enhance your English communication skills.

Coordinating Conjunctions

Coordinating conjunctions, often remembered by the acronym FANBOYS (For, And, Nor, But, Or, Yet, So), play a crucial role in joining words, phrases, or independent clauses. They help create clear and coherent sentences by establishing relationships between different parts of a sentence.

Understanding the FANBOYS:
- For: Expresses a reason or purpose. Example: "She studied diligently, for she wanted to excel in her exams."
- And: Adds information or combines elements. Example: "I enjoy reading novels and watching movies."
- Nor: Connects two negative alternatives. Example: "She neither likes coffee nor tea."
- But: Indicates a contrast or contradiction. Example: "He is intelligent, but he lacks confidence."
- Or: Presents alternatives or choices. Example: "You can have tea or coffee."
- Yet: Introduces a contrast or unexpected result. Example: "She studied hard, yet she didn't perform well in the test."
- So: Indicates a consequence or result. Example: "The weather was cold, so they decided to stay indoors."

Tips for Using Coordinating Conjunctions:

- Equal Importance: Coordinating conjunctions connect elements of equal importance. Ensure that the parts you are connecting have similar grammatical structures.
- Punctuation: When joining independent clauses, use a comma before the coordinating conjunction. Example: "She enjoys hiking, but she doesn't like camping."
- Avoid Comma Splices: Be cautious not to create comma splices (joining two independent clauses with just a comma). If the clauses are closely related, consider using a semicolon or separating them into distinct sentences.
- Vary Your Conjunctions: While FANBOYS are essential, exploring other conjunctions can add variety to your writing. Experiment with subordinating conjunctions for more complex sentence structures.

By mastering coordinating conjunctions, you'll enhance your ability to construct clear and sophisticated sentences. Practice incorporating these conjunctions into your writing and speech to strengthen your overall English proficiency.

Subordinating Conjunctions

Mastering subordinating conjunctions is crucial for constructing complex and varied sentences. Subordinating conjunctions are words that join an independent clause (a complete sentence) with a dependent clause (an incomplete thought). These conjunctions help establish relationships between ideas and clarify the hierarchy of information in a sentence.

Understanding the role of subordinating conjunctions is essential for building more complex and nuanced sentences in English. This section will explore the significance of these conjunctions and provide practical guidance on their usage.

Subordinating conjunctions are words that connect dependent clauses to independent clauses, creating complex sentences. They introduce adverbial clauses that provide additional information, such as time, cause, condition, or contrast.

Common Subordinating Conjunctions

Explore a comprehensive list of commonly used subordinating conjunctions, including but not limited to:

- Time: after, before, when, while, as soon as
- Cause: because, since, as
- Condition: if, unless, whether
- Contrast: although, though, while, whereas

Sentence Structures with Subordinating Conjunctions

Learn how to construct sentences using subordinating conjunctions, emphasizing the proper placement of clauses and maintaining clarity. Examples and exercises will reinforce comprehension.

Understand the punctuation rules associated with subordinating conjunctions. Learn when to use commas, and when they are not necessary, to ensure accurate expression of ideas.

Remember, practice is key to mastering subordinating conjunctions. Regular application of these concepts will lead to increased confidence and proficiency in constructing complex English sentences.

Correlative Conjunctions

Understanding and employing correlative conjunctions is a crucial step towards achieving fluency in English. These conjunctions, working in pairs to connect words, phrases, or clauses, play a pivotal role in conveying complex relationships between ideas. In this section, we will delve into the world of correlative conjunctions, breaking down their usage and providing practical examples to help you grasp their nuances effortlessly.

Correlative conjunctions are pairs of words that work together to link equivalent sentence elements. Common examples include "either...or," "neither...nor," "both...and," "not only...but also," and "whether...or." By mastering these pairs, you will enhance your ability to express contrasts, similarities, alternatives, and additional information in your English communication.

Usage and Examples

Either...or: This conjunction is used to present alternatives. For instance, "You can either attend the meeting today or join the workshop tomorrow."

Neither...nor: To convey the idea of negation for multiple elements, use "neither...nor." Example: "Neither the manager nor the team members were aware of the changes."

Both...and: Use this conjunction to highlight the inclusion of two elements. For example, "She is both intelligent and hardworking."

Not only...but also: This conjunction emphasizes the addition of another noteworthy point. "Not only did he complete the project on time, but also exceeded expectations."

Whether...or: When presenting alternatives or possibilities, "whether...or" is the appropriate choice. Example: "I am unsure whether he will come to the party or stay at home."

Guidelines for Effective Use

Maintain Parallel Structure: Ensure that the elements connected by correlative conjunctions are structurally parallel. This creates clarity and improves the overall flow of your sentences.

Consider the Context: Select the appropriate correlative conjunction based on the specific relationship you intend to convey. Understanding the context is crucial for accurate usage.

Practice, Practice, Practice: Incorporate correlative conjunctions into your everyday communication and writing. The more you practice, the more natural their usage will become.

By mastering correlative conjunctions, you unlock a powerful tool for expressing ideas with precision and sophistication. As you progress in your English language journey, applying these conjunctions will become second nature, allowing you to communicate with confidence and clarity.

CHAPTER 8: Forming Questions and Negations

Forming questions and negations in English involves using specific word order, auxiliary verbs, and other linguistic elements. Here are some general guidelines for forming questions and negations:

Question Words and Structure

Understanding how to form and ask questions is a crucial skill in mastering the English language. Questions play a vital role in communication, allowing you to seek information, express curiosity, and engage in meaningful conversations. In this section, we will delve into the essential question words and structures to help you navigate the world of English inquiries with confidence.

1. Question Words: Who, What, Where, When, Why, and How

Begin by familiarizing yourself with the primary question words: Who, What, Where, When, Why, and How. These words serve as the foundation for constructing various types of questions. Let's explore each one:

Who: Used to inquire about people.
Example: Who is coming to the party tonight?

What: Employed to ask about things, actions, or ideas.
Example: What is your favorite movie?

Where: Aids in questioning the location or place.
Example: Where did you spend your last vacation?

When: Seeks information about time.
Example: When is your birthday?

Why: Used to understand the reason or purpose.
Example: Why did you choose this career?

How: Inquires about the manner or method.
Example: How do you cook pasta?

2. Question Structures

Understanding the structure of questions is equally important. In English, the basic structure for yes/no questions involves inverting the subject and auxiliary verb. For example:

Statement: You are coming to the event.
Yes/No Question: Are you coming to the event?

When using question words, the structure changes slightly. Consider the following:
Statement: She is going to the market.
Wh- Question: Where is she going?

By mastering these structures, you'll be able to form questions effectively, enhancing your ability to communicate and understand others.
Apply your knowledge in real-life situations. Practice asking questions in everyday conversations, whether it's at work, with friends, or in social settings. The more you integrate question words into your language usage, the more natural they will become.
Mastering question words and structure is a key step towards fluency in English. Embrace the learning process, practice consistently, and soon you'll find yourself navigating conversations with ease.

Negation in Statements and Questions

Questions:
Yes/No Questions:
Invert the subject and auxiliary verb.
Example: She is going to the store. -> Is she going to the store?

Wh-Questions:
Use question words (who, what, where, when, why, how) to begin the question.
Example: He is reading a book. -> What is he reading?

To Be Questions:
Invert the subject and the verb "to be."
Example: They are at the park. -> Are they at the park?

Modal Verb Questions:
Invert the subject and the modal verb.
Example: She can swim. -> Can she swim?

Negations in Statements:
Negation with "Not":
Add "not" after the auxiliary verb.
Example: I am happy. -> I am not happy.

Negation with "To Be":
Add "not" after the verb "to be."
Example: They are here. -> They are not here.

Negation with Modal Verbs:
Add "not" after the modal verb.
Example: He can help. -> He cannot help.

Negation with Present Simple and Past Simple:
Use "do not" (don't) or "does not" (doesn't) for present simple. Use "did not" (didn't) for past simple.

Example (Present Simple): I like coffee. -> I do not like coffee (I don't like coffee).
Example (Past Simple): She went to the store. -> She did not go to the store (She didn't go to the store).

Remember that the specific structure may vary depending on the tense and the type of verb used in the sentence. Always consider the context and the type of question or negation you are forming.

CHAPTER 9: Essential English Grammar Structures

Understanding essential English grammar structures is crucial for effective communication. Here are some key grammar structures:

Active vs. Passive Voice

Understanding and employing active and passive voice is a crucial aspect of mastering the English language. In this section, we will explore the differences between active and passive voice and learn how to use them effectively in your writing and communication.

Active Voice

Active voice is a sentence or clause in which the subject performs the action. It is straightforward, direct, and often more engaging. In active voice, the focus is on the doer of the action.
Example:
The chef prepared a delicious meal for the guests.
Here, "the chef" is the doer of the action, and the sentence is clear and concise.

Passive Voice

Passive voice, on the other hand, occurs when the subject is the receiver of the action rather than the doer. While passive voice can be useful in certain contexts, it is generally considered less direct and can sometimes make sentences more complicated.
Example:
A delicious meal was prepared for the guests by the chef.

In this passive construction, the emphasis is on "a delicious meal" rather than the chef. Passive voice is often used when the doer of the action is unknown, unimportant, or when the writer wants to shift the focus.
Deciding whether to use active or passive voice depends on the context and what you want to emphasize. Active voice is typically preferred for its clarity and directness, making it the go-to choice in most situations. However, passive voice can be appropriate when the emphasis is on the receiver of the action or when the doer is less important.

Mastering active and passive voice is an essential step in becoming proficient in English. By understanding when and how to use each, you'll not only improve your writing but also enhance your overall communication skills.

Direct and Indirect Speech

Communication is a vital aspect of language, and mastering the art of expressing thoughts and statements is crucial for effective English language usage. In this section, we delve into the intricacies of direct and indirect speech, offering you a comprehensive guide to navigate through these forms with confidence.

Understanding Direct Speech

Direct speech involves quoting the exact words spoken by a person, and it is often used to add authenticity and immediacy to your writing or dialogue. In direct speech, the speaker's words are enclosed within quotation marks. For example:

Direct Speech:

She said, "I will meet you at the park at 3 o'clock."

In this instance, the exact words spoken by the person are conveyed within the quotation marks, preserving the original expression.

Mastering Indirect Speech

Indirect speech, on the other hand, involves paraphrasing or reporting what someone has said without quoting their exact words. When transforming direct speech into indirect speech, it is important to consider changes in pronouns, tenses, and time expressions. For example:

Direct Speech:	**Indirect Speech:**
She said, "I will meet you at the park at 3 o'clock."	She said that she would meet me at the park at 3 o'clock.

Notice the shift in pronouns and tenses when converting the statement from direct to indirect speech. Mastery of these transformations is essential for clear and accurate communication.

Direct Speech:	John mentioned that he loves studying
John said, "I love studying languages."	languages.
Indirect Speech:	

To truly master direct and indirect speech, practice is key. Engage in exercises that involve transforming sentences from direct to indirect speech and vice versa. This hands-on approach will solidify your understanding and enhance your ability to use both forms fluently.

Remember that mastering direct and indirect speech opens doors to effective communication and polished language skills. Embrace the challenge, practice consistently, and watch your command over these speech forms grow.

CHAPTER 10: Review & Practice: Grammar Mastery Exercises

Exercise 1:

Choose the appropriate options from the statements below:

Mr. Lin followed __ and ____ son out of the grocery store. (A. him, his B. he, his)

Answer: A

Alan then chased __ and __ daughter out of his house. (A. her, her B. she, her C. he, him)

Answer: A

He gave ____ a good handshake after the presentation. (A. he B. his C. him)

Answer: C

The man confessed it was ____ who robbed the lady. (A. him B. he C. his)

Answer: B

I have told ____ to move out. (A. they B. them)

Answer: B

Exercise 2:

Read the following dialogue and fill in the blank with the words from the box. Two words in the box will not be used. You can use each word more than once.

is	am	are	that	this	'm not	those

A: Hi, my name _____ Andrea. What _____ your name?

B: I _____ Bobby. Nice to meet you Andrea. Where _____ you from?

A: California, but my parents _____ from Mexico. And you?

B: I _____ from New York.

A: How old _____ you?

B: I _____ 23 years old, but my birthday _____ next week and then I'll be 24.

A: Nice. I _____ 23 also. _____ you a student?

B: No, I _____. I _____ an engineer. What about you?

A: I'm a student here. My sister _____ a student here too. _____'s her over there.

B: _____ she older than you?

A: No, she _____ younger. _____ those your books?

B: Yes, they are. _____ the library open? I need to return some books.

A: Yes, it _____. I'll go with you.

Answers

A: Hi, my name ....*is*......... Andrea. What ....*is*........your name?

B: I ....*am*....... Bobby. Nice to meet you Andrea. Where ....*are*.......... you from?

A: California, but my parents ....*are*............ from Mexico. Any you?

B: I ....*am*......... from New York.

A: How old ....*are*............ you?

B: I ....*am*......... 23 years old, but my birthday ....*is*.............. next week and then I'll be 24.

A: Nice. I ....*am*........... 23 also. ....*Are*.................. you a student?

B: No, I .....*'m not*.............. I ....*am*............. an engineer. What about you?

A: I'm a student here. My sister ....*is* ....a student here too. .....*That*.....'s her over there.

B: ....*Is*...........she older than you?

A: No, she ....*is*............ younger. ....*Are*............. those your books?

B: Yes, they are. ....*Is*.............. the library open? I need to return some books.

A: Yes, it ....*is*.......... I'll go with you.

Exercise 3:

Choose the appropriate options from the statements below:

Are your dresses _____ shorter these days? (A. More B. much)

Answer: B

A

There is too _____ noise in the air. (A. much B. many)

Answer: A

I have ____ worries than you do. (A. less B. fewer)

Answer: B

We will go out _____. (A. next Friday B. Friday next)

Answer: A

____ question in the script carries equal marks. (A. Every B. Each)

Answer: B

Dad gave me _____ money to spend at school. (A. little B. a little C. few D. small)

Answer: B

Tell me the ____ news. (A. last B. latest)

Answer: B

The _____ of the story was emphasized. (A. important B. importance)

Answer: B

Exercise 4:

Use the words below to make questions using the "be" verb. Then, answer the questions, or practice asking and answering the questions with a partner.

Example: Name?

Answer: What is your name? (My name is...)

- Name?
- From?
- Nationality?
- Age?
- Married?
- Single?

- A student?   • your job?

Answers

Name? What is your name? (My name is. . .)
From? Where are you from? (I'm from. . .)
Nationality? What is your nationality? (My nationality is. . .)
Age? How old are you? (I am. . . years old)
Married? Are you married? (Yes, I am. /No, I'm not.)
Single? Are you single? (Yes, I am. /No, I'm not.)
A student? Are you a student? (Yes, I am. / No, I'm not.)
your job? What is your job? (I'm a . . .)

Exercise 5:

Fill in the blank with the correct form of the "be" verb.
He _____ not here right now.
We _____ students at this university.
_____ I late?
Those girls _____ not part of my group.
That computer _____ expensive.

Answers

He ....*is*..... not here right now.
We ....*are*..... students at this university.
....*Am*.... I late?
Those girls .....*are*..... not part of my group.
That computer ....*is*....... expensive.

Exercise 6:

Choose the appropriate options from the statements below:
He stepped _____ the house. (A. out B. outside C. in)
Answer: B
He flew ____ of town. (A. out B. outside C. away)
Answer: A
____ 30th of January marks our wedding anniversary. (A. The B. In C. At)
Answer: A
We shall hang out _____ 6 o'clock tomorrow. (A. on B. at C. in)
Answer: B
They'll meet ____ five minutes. (A. at B. in)
Answer: B

Exercise 7:

Use the following words to create questions using the 'be' verb

(you/ hungry)

(how old/ he)

(what/ that)

(where /my shoes)

(when/ their birthdays)

Answers

(you/ hungry) Are you hungry?

(how old/ he) How old is he?

(what/ that) What is that?

(where /my shoes) Where are my shoes?

(when/ their birthdays) When are their birthdays?

BOOK 2: ENGLISH VERBS IN ACTION

CHAPTER 11: Introduction: The Versatility of Verbs

Have you ever marveled at the dynamic dance of language, where mere words possess the power to shape our thoughts, express our deepest emotions, and propel us into action? Welcome to "English Verbs in Action," a journey into the heartbeat of the English language. In the vast tapestry of linguistic expression, verbs stand as the vibrant threads that weave together the narratives of our lives. They are the engines of communication, propelling us forward with every sentence, every story, and every conversation.

This book is an exploration of the multifaceted world of English verbs, those versatile tools that not only convey action but also paint vivid pictures of experiences, emotions, and relationships. As we embark on this linguistic adventure, we will delve into the nuances of verb usage, dissecting the ways in which these words breathe life into our everyday interactions.

Join me in unlocking the secrets behind the verbs that shape our language and, by extension, our understanding of the world. Let's discover the beauty, power, and versatility of English verbs as they come to life in the rich tapestry of human communication.

In the vast realm of the English language, verbs stand as the dynamic powerhouses, breathing life into sentences and giving them movement and vitality. Understanding the versatility of verbs is a crucial step in mastering the art of English communication. So, let's delve into the world of verbs and explore their multifaceted nature.

1. Action Verbs:
These are the verbs that depict a physical or mental action. From "run" to "think," action verbs infuse your sentences with energy, allowing you to vividly describe activities and thoughts. Practice incorporating action verbs into your everyday conversations to make your speech more dynamic and engaging.
Example: Sarah runs in the morning to stay fit.

2. Helping Verbs:
Also known as auxiliary verbs, helping verbs work in conjunction with the main verb to express nuances such as possibility, obligation, or time. Understanding the interplay between helping verbs and main verbs is key to constructing grammatically correct sentences.
Example: I have completed my assignment.

3. Linking Verbs:

These verbs connect the subject of a sentence to a subject complement, usually an adjective or a noun. Common linking verbs include "am," "is," "are," "was," and "were." Mastering linking verbs is essential for describing states of being and forming coherent sentences.

Example: The flowers are beautiful.

4. Modal Verbs:

Modal verbs convey a sense of possibility, necessity, or permission. Examples include "can," "could," "may," "might," "shall," "should," "will," and "would." Learning how to use modal verbs enhances your ability to express varying degrees of certainty and obligation.

Example: You can join us if you want.

5. Transitive and Intransitive Verbs:

Verbs can be classified based on the type of action they perform. Transitive verbs take a direct object, while intransitive verbs do not. Recognizing this distinction is vital for constructing grammatically sound sentences.

Transitive Verb Example: She ate the delicious cake.

Intransitive Verb Example: The cat slept peacefully.

As you embark on your English learning journey, embrace the versatility of verbs. Experiment with different verb forms and structures to convey your thoughts effectively. The more you immerse yourself in the world of verbs, the more confident and articulate you will become in expressing yourself in English.

CHAPTER 12: 50 Essential English Verbs

Learning verbs is a fundamental step in mastering any language, and English is no exception. Verbs are the action words that give life to our sentences, describing what we do in our daily lives. In this section, we will explore 50 essential English verbs divided into Daily Activities verbs and Work and Leisure Verbs.

Daily Activities

In this section, we will explore 25 essential English verbs that are commonly used in various daily activities. Understanding and incorporating these verbs into your vocabulary will significantly enhance your ability to communicate effectively in English.

- Eat: Start your day by learning how to express the act of consuming food. "I eat breakfast every morning."
- Drink: Stay hydrated and express this essential action. "She drinks a cup of tea in the afternoon."
- Sleep: Discuss your daily rest routine. "They sleep for eight hours every night."
- Work: Communicate your employment activities. "He works in an office from 9 to 5."
- Study: Describe your academic pursuits. "We study English for an hour every day."
- Read: Share your reading habits. "She reads a book before bedtime."
- Write: Express your thoughts on paper. "I write in my journal every evening."
- Talk: Communicate verbally with others. "They talk about their day during dinner."
- Listen: Pay attention to sounds and conversations. "We listen to music while driving."
- Watch: Observe visual content. "He watches movies on weekends."
- Cook: Prepare meals in the kitchen. "She cooks dinner for her family."
- Clean: Keep your living space tidy. "We clean the house every Saturday."
- Exercise: Stay active and healthy. "They exercise at the gym three times a week."
- Shop: Purchase goods and services. "I shop for groceries every Sunday."
- Drive: Operate a vehicle. "He drives to work every day."
- Walk: Move on foot. "She walks her dog in the park."
- Run: Move at a faster pace. "I run for exercise in the morning."
- Play: Engage in recreational activities. "They play tennis on weekends."
- Dance: Move rhythmically to music. "We dance at parties for fun."
- Sing: Produce musical sounds with your voice. "She sings in the choir."
- Travel: Journey to different places. "He travels for work frequently."
- Plan: Organize and arrange activities. "We plan our schedule for the week."
- Meet: Encounter and interact with people. "They meet friends for coffee."

- Relax: Take a break and unwind. "I relax by reading a book."
- Enjoy: Find pleasure in various activities. "She enjoys spending time outdoors."

Practice using these verbs in sentences to reinforce your understanding and improve your English communication skills. As you become familiar with these essential verbs, you'll find yourself expressing your daily activities with confidence.

Work and Leisure

Here's a list of 25 work-related verbs:

- Communicate: Expressing ideas and information clearly.
- Collaborate: Working together with others to achieve a common goal.
- Organize: Arranging tasks or items in a systematic manner.
- Prioritize: Deciding the order of importance for tasks or activities.
- Delegate: Assigning responsibilities to others.
- Problem-Solve: Finding solutions to challenges or issues.
- Adapt: Adjusting to changes in the work environment.
- Innovate: Introducing new ideas or methods.
- Negotiate: Discussing and reaching agreements with others.
- Lead: Guiding and directing a team or group.
- Manage: Overseeing and coordinating tasks or projects.
- Motivate: Encouraging and inspiring others to achieve their best.
- Evaluate: Assessing the performance or effectiveness of something.
- Plan: Creating a detailed strategy or course of action.
- Train: Instructing others to develop specific skills.
- Research: Gathering information for a particular purpose.
- Implement: Putting a plan or decision into action.
- Coordinate: Harmonizing various elements to work together smoothly.
- Supervise: Monitoring and overseeing the work of others.
- Review: Examining or assessing something critically.
- Meet: Assemble or gather for a specific purpose.
- Document: Recording information in writing or other formats.
- Present: Sharing information or ideas in a formal setting.
- Network: Building and maintaining professional connections.
- Achieve: Attaining goals or objectives.

CHAPTER 13: Verb Conjugation Simplified

Verb conjugation is the process of changing a verb to agree with its subject in terms of person, number, gender, tense, aspect, mood, and voice. While verb conjugation can be complex in some languages, I'll simplify it for you using English as an example.

Regular Verb Patterns

In English, verbs play a crucial role in expressing actions, states, or occurrences. Understanding verb patterns is fundamental to mastering the language. Regular verbs follow specific patterns when conjugated in different tenses. This section will guide you through the common patterns associated with regular verbs, making your journey to English proficiency smoother.

Infinitive Form

The base form of a verb, known as the infinitive, is the simplest and most generic way to express an action. In English, infinitives are often identified by the word "to" followed by the base verb. For example: "to walk," "to talk," and "to study."

Simple Present Tense

Regular verbs in the simple present tense are straightforward to conjugate. In most cases, you simply add "-s" or "-es" to the base form when the subject is third person singular (he, she, it).

Example:

- I walk to school every day.
- She talks to her friends on the phone.
- The cat sleeps in the afternoon.

Simple Past Tense

To form the simple past tense of regular verbs, add "-ed" to the base form. This rule applies to most regular verbs, making past tense conjugation relatively consistent.

Example:

- I walked to the store yesterday.
- They talked about their weekend.
- He played the piano for hours.

Future Tense

Creating the future tense with regular verbs is relatively easy. Simply use the modal verb "will" followed by the base form of the verb.

Example:

- I will walk to the park tomorrow.
- She will talk to her boss about the project.
- They will study for the exam tonight.

Remember: use an "e" in the –ed (past simple and "–ed" form) of regular verbs. And, when you have regular verbs where the vowel changes from "I" to "a" to "u," use "a" in the past simple and "u" in the "-ed" form.

Incorrect: She *enjoy* the movie.
I was very thirsty so I *drunk* water.

Correct: She *enjoyed* the movie.   (past simple)
I was very thirsty so I *drank* water.   (past simple)

Understanding these regular verb patterns is a key step towards building your English language skills. As you practice and use these patterns in your conversations and writing, you'll gain confidence and fluency in expressing yourself in various tenses. Remember, consistency and practice are the keys to success in learning English.

Tackling Irregular Verbs

Learning English verbs can be a challenging task, especially when it comes to irregular verbs. Unlike regular verbs, which follow a predictable pattern when conjugated, irregular verbs have unique forms that don't adhere to the standard rules. However, fear not! In this section, we'll break down the complexities of irregular verbs, making them more manageable and understandable for adult beginners.

Irregular verbs are an essential aspect of English grammar, adding nuance and variety to the language. While regular verbs typically end in "-ed" in their past tense forms, irregular verbs require a bit more memorization. These verbs don't follow a consistent pattern, so it's crucial to familiarize yourself with their different forms.
Start by focusing on a set of common irregular verbs. These include verbs like "be," "have," "do," "go," and "eat." Recognizing these verbs and understanding their irregularities will serve as a solid foundation for tackling more complex ones in the future.

Watch out for irregular verbs that have base form "-d" and past tense "-t" such as:
Incorrect:He *spend* millions of dollars on the surgery.
Correct:He *spent* millions of dollars on the surgery.

Do not use regular past simple "-ed" form for irregular verbs.
Incorrect: He *spended* weeks before coming.
Correct: He *spent* weeks before coming.
Some prepositional words (e.g., about, for, and in) are not used with some verbs used in certain forms.
Incorrect: The school board *discussed about* expelling the student.
Correct: The school board *discussed* expelling the student.

There are prepositional words that fit with prepositional verbs, e.g., lie under, listen to, depend on, wait on, etc.

Incorrect: I like to *listen* him speak.

Correct: I like to *listen to* him speak.

Incorrect: He loves to *wait upon* his parents.

Correct: He loves to *wait on* his parents.

To make learning irregular verbs easier, employ effective memorization techniques. Flashcards, mnemonic devices, and repetition can be valuable tools. Create flashcards with the base form, past tense, and past participle of each irregular verb. Review them regularly to reinforce your memory.

Apply these irregular verbs in context through practice exercises. Construct sentences and engage in conversations that incorporate these verbs. The more you use them, the more natural they will become in your speech and writing.

Take advantage of online resources that offer interactive exercises and quizzes specifically designed for mastering irregular verbs. Many websites and language learning apps provide engaging activities to reinforce your understanding and application of irregular verbs.

Irregular verbs can be tricky, so consistent review is essential. Regularly revisit your list of irregular verbs and practice their usage. Over time, you'll find that these irregularities become second nature, boosting your overall confidence in English communication.

Tackling irregular verbs may seem daunting at first, but with a systematic approach and regular practice, you'll soon find yourself navigating through them effortlessly. Remember, learning a language is a gradual process, and each step you take brings you closer to mastery. Embrace the challenge, stay consistent, and watch your proficiency in irregular verbs grow as you progress on your journey to mastering English.

CHAPTER 14: Advanced Tense Usage

Mastering Perfect and Continuous Forms

In your journey to mastering English, it's essential to understand and utilize the perfect and continuous verb forms effectively. These forms not only add nuance to your expressions but also help convey the precise timing and duration of actions. Let's delve into the intricacies of perfect and continuous tenses to elevate your language skills.

Perfect Tenses: Expressing Completed Actions

Perfect tenses indicate actions that are completed before a specific point in time or before another action. There are three primary perfect tenses in English: present perfect, past perfect, and future perfect.

Present Perfect (have/has + past participle):
Example: I have lived in this city for five years.
This tense connects the past with the present, emphasizing the relevance of the action to the current moment.

Past Perfect (had + past participle):
Example: She had already finished her work when I arrived.
Used to express an action completed before another past action, highlighting the sequence of events.

Future Perfect (will have + past participle):
Example: By next year, he will have graduated from college.
Indicates an action that will be completed before a specific future point.

Continuous Tenses: Emphasizing Duration

Continuous tenses, also known as progressive tenses, convey actions that are ongoing or in progress. There are three main continuous tenses: present continuous, past continuous, and future continuous.

Present Continuous (am/is/are + present participle):
Example: They are studying for their exams.
Highlights an action that is happening at the current moment.

Past Continuous (was/were + present participle):
Example: She was reading a book when the phone rang.
Describes an ongoing action interrupted by another event in the past.

Future Continuous (will be + present participle):
Example: This time tomorrow, we will be exploring the city.
Indicates an ongoing action at a specific future point.

Perfect Continuous Tenses: Combining Duration and Completion
Perfect continuous tenses combine the aspects of both perfect and continuous tenses, emphasizing both the duration and completion of an action.

Present Perfect Continuous (have/has been + present participle):
Example: They have been working on the project for three hours.
Highlights the duration of an action that started in the past and continues into the present.

Past Perfect Continuous (had been + present participle):
Example: By noon, she had been waiting for over an hour.
Indicates the duration of an action that was ongoing before another past action.

Future Perfect Continuous (will have been + present participle):
Example: By the time you arrive, I will have been cooking dinner for an hour.
Conveys the duration of an action that will be ongoing before a specific future point.

By mastering these perfect and continuous forms, you'll enhance your ability to express yourself accurately in various time frames. Practice these tenses in context to solidify your understanding and become proficient in using them effortlessly.

The Conditional and Subjunctive Moods

Understanding the conditional and subjunctive moods in English can elevate your language skills to a more advanced level. These moods add nuances to expressing possibilities, hypothetical situations, desires, doubts, and more. In this section, we'll break down the key concepts of the conditional and subjunctive moods to help you use them confidently in your conversations.

1. The Conditional Mood: Expressing Possibilities
The conditional mood is often used to talk about hypothetical situations, potential outcomes, or events that depend on certain conditions. In English, the conditional is formed using the modal verb "would" or "could" with the base form of the main verb.
Example: If I had more time, I would learn to play the guitar.
Learn to recognize common conditional structures and practice incorporating them into your speech. This will enable you to discuss hypothetical scenarios with ease.

2. The Subjunctive Mood: Conveying Desires, Suggestions, and Doubts

The subjunctive mood is employed to express desires, suggestions, recommendations, doubts, or hypothetical situations that are contrary to reality. While the subjunctive mood doesn't always result in a noticeable change in verb form, it is crucial for conveying a specific tone or intention.

Example: It is essential that she be present at the meeting.

Explore different contexts where the subjunctive mood is used, such as expressing wishes, making suggestions, or stating hypothetical conditions. Practice recognizing when to use the subjunctive for clearer and more nuanced communication.

3. Common Triggers for Subjunctive Mood

Certain phrases and expressions often signal the use of the subjunctive mood. These include:

Wishes and desires: I wish, If only, I'd rather
Suggestions and recommendations: It's important, It's crucial, It's necessary
Doubts and hypothetical situations: If it were, I doubt, Suppose that
Familiarize yourself with these triggers to identify opportunities for incorporating the subjunctive mood into your sentences.

Mastering the conditional and subjunctive moods is a significant step toward achieving fluency in English. Embrace these nuances, practice consistently, and soon you'll find yourself expressing ideas with precision and sophistication.

CHAPTER 15: Verbs in Context

Everyday Conversations

In this section, we will focus on practical language skills that are essential for navigating everyday conversations. The ability to communicate effectively in common situations is crucial for adult beginners learning English. Whether you're at work, in a social setting, or handling daily tasks, mastering these conversational skills will greatly enhance your language proficiency.

1. Greetings and Introductions:

Begin by mastering the art of greetings. Learn how to say "hello," "hi," and other common expressions. Practice introducing yourself and asking others for their names. Understanding the cultural nuances of greetings is also important, as it varies from one English-speaking community to another.

2. Small Talk:

Engaging in small talk is a skill that opens doors to meaningful connections. Practice discussing topics like the weather, current events, or common interests. Learn to ask open-ended questions and share your thoughts in a concise manner. Small talk serves as a foundation for more in-depth conversations.

3. Expressing Likes and Dislikes:

Being able to express your preferences is essential in daily conversations. Practice using phrases like "I like," "I don't like," "I enjoy," and "I prefer." This will help you communicate your tastes, allowing for more personalized and engaging interactions.

4. Giving and Receiving Directions:

Navigate the challenges of daily life by mastering the language of directions. Practice asking for and giving directions using common phrases. Whether you're in a new neighborhood or seeking guidance within a building, understanding and using directional language is key.

5. Making Plans:

Learn to make plans and arrangements effectively. Practice suggesting activities, setting dates and times, and confirming plans. This will not only enhance your conversational skills but also empower you to actively participate in social activities.

6. Handling Common Situations:

Prepare for everyday scenarios by practicing relevant vocabulary and expressions. Whether you're at a restaurant, in a store, or dealing with service professionals, being able to communicate your needs and understand responses is crucial.

7. Politeness and Etiquette:

Mastering polite language and cultural etiquette is fundamental in English communication. Practice saying "please," "thank you," and other polite expressions appropriately. Understand cultural norms to ensure respectful and effective communication.

Speak the following sentence **politely**:

1. Can you please help me?
2. Can I use your mobile for two minutes?
3. Could you please tell me this address?
4. Can you please shut the door?
5. Can I come with you?
6. May I call you after ten minutes?
7. Can I go through this report?
8. Could you please stop smoking?
9. Where can I park my car?
10. Would you like to pay by cash or card?
11. Would you like to meet my boss?

Remember, mastering everyday conversations is a gradual process. Consistent practice, exposure to real-life situations, and a willingness to learn from mistakes will contribute to your overall language development. As you progress through this section, embrace opportunities to apply these skills in your daily life, and watch your confidence in English conversation grow.

Workplace and Formal Settings

In the professional world, effective communication is paramount. Whether you are interacting with colleagues, clients, or superiors, mastering workplace and formal settings conversations is essential for success. This section will guide you through the key aspects of communication in these contexts.

1. Understanding Workplace Etiquette:

Learn the nuances of workplace etiquette, such as appropriate greetings and gestures.
Understand the importance of punctuality and how it contributes to a positive professional image.

2. Developing Polite Language:

Master the art of using polite language to convey ideas and opinions respectfully.
Practice expressing disagreement tactfully without causing offense.

3. Navigating Formal Introductions:

Gain confidence in introducing yourself and others in formal settings.
Learn to remember and use titles and formal address appropriately.

4. Effective Meeting Participation:

Acquire the skills to actively contribute to meetings, including asking questions and expressing opinions.

Understand the importance of listening actively and taking concise notes during discussions.

5. Polishing Email and Written Communication:

Improve your written communication skills for professional emails and documents.

Learn to structure emails appropriately and use a formal tone when necessary.

6. Handling Difficult Conversations:

Develop strategies for handling sensitive or challenging topics in a professional manner.

Practice active listening and empathy to navigate disagreements with colleagues.

7. Networking in Professional Settings:

Understand the significance of networking in your professional growth.

Learn how to initiate and maintain professional relationships through effective communication.

8. Cultural Sensitivity:

Appreciate and respect cultural differences in communication styles within the workplace.

Gain insights into how cultural nuances can impact professional interactions.

9. Using Formal Vocabulary:

Expand your vocabulary to include formal and workplace-specific terms.

Practice incorporating these words into your everyday conversations and written communication.

10. Continuous Improvement:

Recognize that effective communication is a skill that can always be improved.

Seek feedback from colleagues and superiors to refine your communication style.

By mastering workplace and formal settings conversations, you'll not only enhance your professional standing but also build stronger relationships within your work environment. These skills are invaluable as you progress in your career and engage with diverse professionals in various settings.

CHAPTER 16: Phrasal Verbs Demystified

Phrasal verbs are combinations of a main verb and one or more particles or prepositions. They often have meanings that may not be immediately obvious from the individual words. Learning phrasal verbs is essential for mastering English, as they are commonly used in both spoken and written language. Here are some common types of phrasal verbs and examples to help demystify them:

Common Phrasal Verbs and Their Meanings

Learning English involves not just understanding individual words but also grasping the nuances of phrasal verbs, an essential aspect of the language. Phrasal verbs are combinations of verbs and prepositions or adverbs that form a unique meaning distinct from the individual words. In this chapter, we will delve into mastering common phrasal verbs, providing you with a solid foundation to enhance your language skills.

Unraveling the Structure of Phrasal Verbs

Before we dive into specific phrasal verbs, let's break down their structure. A phrasal verb typically consists of a main verb combined with one or more particles, which can be prepositions or adverbs. Understanding how these components interact is crucial for deciphering the intended meaning. We'll explore examples and exercises to solidify your comprehension.

Building Vocabulary with Everyday Phrasal Verbs

In this section, we will focus on phrasal verbs commonly used in daily conversations. From "break up" to "come across," you'll learn the practical applications of these expressions in various contexts. Through real-life examples, dialogues, and exercises, you'll gain confidence in incorporating these phrasal verbs into your own speech.

Navigating Phrasal Verbs in Different Tenses

Understanding how phrasal verbs function across different tenses is essential for effective communication. This section will guide you through the nuances of using phrasal verbs in past, present, and future tenses. You'll discover how these verbs adapt to convey precise meanings in diverse time frames.

Expressing Emotions and States with Phrasal Verbs

Phrasal verbs play a significant role in expressing emotions and states of being. Whether it's "cheer up" or "give in," these expressions add depth to your language skills. Through interactive exercises and scenarios, you'll learn to convey a wide range of feelings and situations using the appropriate phrasal verbs.

Mastering Phrasal Verbs in Context

The key to fluency lies in using phrasal verbs seamlessly in context. This section will provide you with practical scenarios and dialogues where you can apply the phrasal verbs you've learned.

Through role-playing and interactive exercises, you'll enhance your ability to integrate these expressions naturally into your everyday conversations.

By the end of this chapter, you will have a comprehensive understanding of common phrasal verbs and the confidence to use them effectively. Embrace the journey of mastering these essential elements of English, and watch as your language skills reach new heights.

Usage in Sentences

Welcome to a crucial aspect of English language learning - mastering common phrasal verbs. Phrasal verbs are combinations of verbs and prepositions or adverbs that often carry a meaning different from the individual words. These versatile linguistic tools add nuance and depth to your language skills, making your expressions more natural and fluent.

Phrasal verbs can be challenging for beginners, as their meanings are not always literal. For example, "give up" doesn't mean to physically hand something over; rather, it means to surrender or quit. This section will guide you through the usage of common phrasal verbs, helping you grasp their meanings in context.

To truly master phrasal verbs, it's crucial to learn them in context. We'll provide you with sentences and examples that showcase how these expressions are used in everyday conversation. By understanding the context in which phrasal verbs are employed, you'll be better equipped to integrate them into your own speech.

Here are some examples of sentences with phrasal verbs:
Break up: I had to break up with my partner because we couldn't agree on important issues.
Call off: The organizers decided to call off the event due to bad weather.
Cut down: I need to cut down on sugary snacks to improve my health.
Look forward to: I'm looking forward to meeting my friends at the party tonight.
Turn on: Can you please turn on the lights? It's getting dark in here.
Take off: The plane is scheduled to take off in 30 minutes.
Put off: We had to put off the meeting until next week because of a scheduling conflict.
Give up: Despite facing challenges, she refused to give up on her dreams.
Bring up: It's not easy to bring up difficult topics in a conversation.
Come across: I came across an interesting article while browsing the internet.
Look up: If you don't know the meaning of a word, you can look it up in the dictionary.
Set up: They are planning to set up a new business in the city.

Break down: Unfortunately, the car broke down on our way to the airport.
Hold on: Please hold on for a moment while I check the information.
Get over: It took her a long time to get over the loss of her beloved pet.
Run out of: We ran out of milk, so I need to buy some on the way home.
Put up with: I can't put up with his constant complaining anymore.
Catch up: Let's meet for coffee sometime and catch up on each other's lives.
Show up: I hope everyone will show up for the meeting on time.
Fill in: Can you fill in for me at work tomorrow? I have a doctor's appointment.
These examples showcase the versatility of phrasal verbs in various contexts and how they contribute to the richness of the English language.
Learning phrasal verbs involves practice. We've included exercises throughout this section to reinforce your understanding. Engaging with these exercises will not only help solidify the meanings but also improve your overall command of the English language.
We'll cover a range of common phrasal verbs, such as "look after," "break down," "come across," and many more. Each phrasal verb will be accompanied by example sentences, demonstrating its application in various contexts. This hands-on approach will enhance your ability to incorporate these expressions seamlessly into your conversations.

In addition to providing examples, we'll offer tips on how to use phrasal verbs effectively. Understanding when and how to employ these expressions will not only make you a more confident communicator but also help you sound more like a native speaker.

As you progress through this section, keep in mind that mastering phrasal verbs is a journey toward fluency. Embrace the learning process, practice regularly, and soon you'll find yourself using these expressions effortlessly in your everyday conversations.

CHAPTER 17: Modal Verbs and Their Nuances

Modal verbs are used in combination with other verbs to indicate ability, permission, possibility, or obligation. In many cases, like *must* or *should*, a modal verb can have a variety of meanings and uses.

Modals Part 1: Must / Have to / Need to

Must shows necessity. We usually use **must** when someone makes a rule or law. When you **must** do something, there is no choice.
1. When you travel abroad, you **must** have a passport.
2. You **must** stop at a red light.
3. You **must** speak quietly in the library.

The negative form of **must** is **must not**. However, the meaning of **must not** is prohibition (in other words, **must not** means **don't do that**).
1. You **must not** smoke here.
2. You **must not** pass a red light without stopping.
3. You **must not** shout in the library.

Have to is like **must**. **Have to** shows necessity, and we use **have to** when someone makes a rule or law that we need to follow. **Have to** is softer than *must*, but like *must*, there is no choice.
1. When you travel abroad, you **have to** have a passport.
2. You **have to** stop at a red light.
3. You **have to** speak quietly in the library.

In a negative sentence, **don't have to** is used to talk about what is not necessary. There is no negative form of **must**, so we do not use **don't must**.
1. When you travel from Baltimore to Phoenix, you **don't have to** bring a passport.
2. You **don't have to** stop at a green light.
3. You **don't have to** speak quietly in the library café.

Had to is used to talk about past necessity. There is no past form of *must* to mean necessity.
1. When I traveled abroad, I **had to** have a passport.
2. You **had to** stop at the red light. That's why the police stopped you.
3. You **have to** speak quietly in the library. That's why the librarian scolded us.

Like **must** and **have to**, **need to** is also used to talk about what is necessary. The basic difference between the term **need to** and the terms **must** and **have to** is where the necessity comes from. Generally, with **must** and **have to**, the necessity comes from someone other than ourselves. With **need to**, the necessity comes from ourselves. Compare the following examples:

1. When you travel abroad, you **must** have a passport. *The necessity comes from the law.*
2. You **have to** *be quiet in the library.* The necessity comes from a rule.
3. *I* **need to** *go on a diet.* The necessity comes from myself.

Need to can be used when you (or someone else) make the rules or plan for yourself.
1. I **need to** exercise more.
2. Matt said he **needs to** get a new computer.
3. We **need to** leave by 5:00 p.m. to get to the station on time.

Expressing Ability, Permission, Obligation

In this section, we will delve into the essential aspects of expressing ability, permission, and obligation in English. These elements are crucial for effective communication and are commonly used in various situations. By mastering these concepts, you'll enhance your language skills and gain confidence in expressing yourself accurately.

Expressing Ability
Being able to convey your capabilities is vital in everyday communication. Whether discussing your skills, talents, or what you can do, understanding how to express ability is fundamental. We'll explore the use of modal verbs such as 'can' and 'could' to articulate your proficiency and potential.
Example:
- I can speak three languages.
- She could play the piano when she was five.

Seeking and Granting Permission
Understanding how to ask for permission and grant it appropriately is crucial in diverse social settings. We'll cover polite expressions and phrases that will help you navigate through situations where permission is needed.
Example:
- May I borrow your pen, please?
- Yes, you may.

Expressing Obligation

Being aware of how to communicate duties and responsibilities is key to effective interaction, especially in professional and formal contexts. We'll introduce modal verbs like 'must' and 'should' to convey obligations clearly.

Example:

- Employees must submit their reports by Friday.

- You should complete the assignment before the deadline.

By the end of this section, you will have a solid understanding of how to express your abilities, request and grant permission, and articulate obligations. These skills will contribute significantly to your overall proficiency in English, empowering you to communicate with clarity and precision.

Making Requests and Offers

Communication is the key to connecting with others, and mastering the art of making requests and offers is crucial in any language. In this section, we'll explore essential phrases and strategies to help you confidently express your needs and extend invitations.

1. Polite Requests:

Politeness goes a long way in any language, and English is no exception. When making requests, it's important to use polite language. Here are some common phrases to help you make requests politely:

- Could you please...?
- Would you mind...?
- I was wondering if you could...

- If it's not too much trouble, can you...?

Practice these phrases in various situations to enhance your ability to make requests with courtesy and respect.

2. Direct Requests:

Sometimes, a direct approach is suitable, especially in informal settings. Here are examples of straightforward requests:

- Can you pass me the salt, please?
- Please send me the report by Friday.

- Tell me about your experience with this project.

Balancing politeness and directness will help you navigate different social situations effectively.

3. Making Offers:

Being able to offer help or assistance is equally important. Here are some phrases to master when making offers:

- Can I help you with that?
- Would you like some assistance?
- Let me know if you need anything.
- I'm here to help.

Practicing these phrases will enable you to extend a helping hand and create a positive atmosphere in your conversations.

4. Expressing Desires and Preferences:

Clearly communicating your desires and preferences is crucial for effective communication. Here are phrases to help you express yourself:

- I would prefer...
- I'd like to...
- It would be great if...
- I'm interested in...

Using these expressions will allow you to articulate your needs and desires with clarity.

5. Role-Playing Exercises:

To solidify your skills, engage in role-playing exercises. Practice making requests and offers with a study partner or in front of a mirror. This hands-on approach will boost your confidence and fluency in real-life situations.

Remember, effective communication is a two-way street. By mastering the art of making requests and offers, you'll enhance your ability to connect with others and navigate social situations with ease. Practice regularly, and soon you'll find yourself expressing your needs and extending invitations with confidence and grace.

CHAPTER 18: Challenging Verb Forms

Gerunds and Infinitives

Learning to use gerunds and infinitives correctly is a crucial step in mastering English grammar. Both gerunds and infinitives are verb forms that can function as nouns in a sentence, but they have different structures and uses. In this section, we will explore the distinctions between gerunds and infinitives and provide practical tips to help you use them accurately.

Understanding Gerunds:

A gerund is the -ing form of a verb, and it functions as a noun in a sentence. When a verb takes on the form of a gerund, it expresses an action as a concrete object or idea. For example:

Swimming is my favorite exercise.

In this sentence, "swimming" acts as a noun, representing the activity or idea of swimming.

Mastering Infinitives:

An infinitive is the base form of a verb, typically preceded by "to." Like gerunds, infinitives can function as nouns, expressing actions in a more abstract sense. Consider the following example:

I like to read before bedtime.

Here, "to read" serves as a noun, indicating the general activity of reading.

Choosing Between Gerunds and Infinitives:

The choice between using a gerund or an infinitive depends on the verb that precedes it and the overall structure of the sentence. Some verbs are followed by gerunds, while others are followed by infinitives. There are also verbs that can be followed by either, with a change in meaning. For instance:

I enjoy playing the piano. (gerund - the activity of playing)

I enjoy to play the piano. (infinitive - the idea or concept of playing)

Common Verbs Followed by Gerunds:

Certain verbs are commonly followed by gerunds. These include:

enjoy: I enjoy swimming.

avoid: She avoids eating spicy food.

consider: They are considering moving to a new city.

Common Verbs Followed by Infinitives:

On the other hand, specific verbs are followed by infinitives, such as:

want: I want to learn English.

decide: He decided to travel during the summer.

plan: We plan to visit the museum.

Practice Tips:

Memorize common verb patterns: Recognizing which verbs are typically followed by gerunds or infinitives will enhance your accuracy in using them.

Read extensively: Exposure to various texts will help you internalize correct usage and improve your overall understanding of gerunds and infinitives.

Practice in context: Engage in conversations or writing exercises that require the use of gerunds and infinitives to solidify your grasp of these structures.

By mastering gerunds and infinitives, you'll add depth and precision to your English language skills. Practice consistently, and soon you'll find yourself using these forms effortlessly in both spoken and written communication.

Causatives and Reporting Verbs

In this section, we will delve into the dynamic world of reporting verbs, essential tools in the English language that allow us to convey information, thoughts, and actions in a clear and concise manner. Mastering reporting verbs is a key step towards effective communication, as they help you report speech, thoughts, and actions of others with precision.

Understanding Reporting Verbs:

Reporting verbs are words that we use to report what someone else has said or done. They play a crucial role in written and spoken communication, adding variety and nuance to your language. Whether you're recounting a conversation, summarizing a text, or expressing opinions, reporting verbs are the building blocks of effective communication.

Common Reporting Verbs:

Let's explore a range of reporting verbs that you can incorporate into your everyday English:

- Say: The most basic reporting verb, used for direct speech. "She said, 'I'll be there at 3 PM.'"
- Tell: Often used with a direct object, indicating the person to whom the information is directed. "He told me that the meeting was postponed."
- Inform: Conveys a formal and structured exchange of information. "The manager informed the team about the upcoming changes."
- Explain: Indicates a detailed clarification or elucidation of a concept. "The teacher explained the grammar rules with clarity."

- Suggest: Implies a recommendation or proposal. "She suggested trying a different approach to solve the problem."

To solidify your understanding, engage in practical exercises where you create sentences using different reporting verbs. Consider scenarios such as workplace communication, casual conversations, and academic discussions. This hands-on approach will enhance your ability to choose the most appropriate reporting verb for each situation.

Tips for Effective Usage:
Pay attention to the context and formality of your communication.
Experiment with different reporting verbs to convey varying degrees of certainty or doubt.
Practice incorporating reporting verbs into your writing and speaking to enhance fluency.

CHAPTER 19: Verbs in Professional and Academic English

In professional and academic English, using appropriate verbs is crucial to convey ideas clearly and concisely. Here are some guidelines for choosing effective verbs in these contexts:

Be Specific:

Instead of using general verbs like "do," "make," or "have," opt for more specific verbs that precisely describe the action. For example:

- General: "Make a decision."
- Specific: "Reach a decision."

Use Action Verbs:

Choose strong action verbs that convey a sense of movement and activity. This adds energy and clarity to your writing.

- Weak: "Take into consideration."
- Strong: "Consider."

Avoid Nominalization:

Nominalization is the process of turning verbs into nouns. While it's sometimes necessary, using active verbs often leads to more direct and engaging writing.

- Nominalization: "The completion of the project is the responsibility of the team."
- Active verb: "The team is responsible for completing the project."

Be Consistent:

Maintain consistency in verb tense throughout your writing. Choose the appropriate tense based on the context and the time frame of the actions you are describing.

Be Precise:

Select verbs that precisely convey the intended meaning. For example, instead of "say," you might use "assert," "argue," or "explain" based on the context.

Use Modifiers Wisely:

When needed, incorporate adverbs to modify your verbs and provide additional context. However, avoid overusing adverbs, and ensure they genuinely enhance the meaning of the verb.

- Original: "He spoke loudly."
- Improved: "He asserted his opinion loudly."

Consider Formality:

Adjust the level of formality in your writing by choosing verbs that suit the tone of the document. For academic and professional writing, a more formal tone is usually appropriate.

Vary Your Vocabulary:

Avoid repetition by using a variety of verbs. This not only makes your writing more interesting but also allows you to express different shades of meaning.

Be Mindful of Word Choice:

Choose verbs that accurately reflect the intended action. Pay attention to the nuances of meaning between similar verbs.

Proofread Carefully:

After writing, proofread your work to ensure that verbs are used correctly, and the overall tone and meaning align with your intended message.

Remember, the choice of verbs can significantly impact the clarity, tone, and effectiveness of your writing. Tailor your verb choices to the specific demands of the professional or academic context in which you are communicating.

Business Meetings and Correspondence

In the realm of business, the ability to communicate effectively is not just an advantage; it's a necessity. Mastering the precise use of language, especially verbs, is fundamental in articulating your thoughts with clarity and authority. This segment offers insights into pivotal verbs that are frequently utilized in the context of business meetings and professional correspondence.

1. **Discuss**:
- Example: "We shall discuss the most recent updates on the project in our upcoming meeting."
2. **Present**:
- Example: "In the session tomorrow, I intend to present the quarterly sales analysis."
3. **Suggest**:
- Example: "May I suggest an innovative strategy that could elevate our customer engagement?"
4. **Conclude**:
- Example: "We shall wrap up today's discussion with a rundown of the decided action points."
5. **Inquire**:
- Example: "I'm reaching out to inquire about the current status of our order that is still pending."
6. **Confirm**:
- Example: "Kindly confirm your participation in the workshop designed for team enhancement."
7. **Recommend**:
- Example: "Based on the findings, I firmly recommend we proceed with the suggested modifications to boost efficiency."
8. **Negotiate**:
- Example: "We are willing to engage in discussions to negotiate the conditions of our collaborative agreement."
9. **Update**:
- Example: "I aim to provide you with an update regarding the milestones achieved in the ongoing initiative."

10. **Request**:
- Example: "I am penning this to officially request your support in the meticulous audit that is scheduled."

Utilize these verbs judiciously, tailoring your language to the situation at hand. Whether steering a pivotal meeting or composing a critical email, the judicious choice of verbs will magnify the efficacy of your communication, ensuring your professionalism shines through.

As you incorporate these verbs into varied business scenarios, your proficiency in delivering your message with precision and professionalism will undoubtedly flourish. Continue refining your communicative prowess, and you will seamlessly navigate through the intricacies of business meetings and correspondence.

Academic Writing and Discussions

In the realm of academic communication, verbs play a pivotal role in conveying precise meaning and establishing a strong connection between ideas. This section is dedicated to unraveling the intricacies of using verbs effectively in both writing and discussions within an academic context. By mastering the nuances of verbs, you will enhance your ability to express thoughts with clarity and sophistication.

1. Choosing the Right Verbs:
In academic writing, the choice of verbs can significantly impact the overall quality of your work. Opt for strong and specific verbs that convey your intended meaning with precision. Avoid generic verbs that may weaken the impact of your statements. For instance, instead of using "make" or "do," consider employing verbs like "formulate," "execute," or "synthesize" to provide a clearer picture of your actions.

2. Active Voice vs. Passive Voice:
Understanding when to use the active voice and when to employ the passive voice is crucial in academic writing. While the active voice is direct and emphasizes the doer of the action, the passive voice shifts the focus to the recipient of the action. Strive for a balance between the two, recognizing that the active voice often enhances clarity and engagement.

3. Verb Tenses and Consistency:
Correctly utilizing verb tenses ensures coherence in your writing. Be mindful of shifting between past, present, and future tenses, and maintain consistency throughout your work. Consider the temporal context of your statements and choose the appropriate tense to convey the timeline of events or ideas.

'4. Precision in Discussions:

In academic discussions, verbs serve as the backbone of effective communication. Whether participating in a seminar or engaging in a group discussion, selecting the right verbs will amplify the impact of your contributions. Expressing ideas concisely and vividly will not only enhance your understanding but also contribute to a more dynamic and engaging conversation.

5. Academic Conventions:

Familiarize yourself with the specific verb usage conventions within your academic discipline. Different fields may have unique preferences for expressing actions and concepts. Consult reputable academic sources in your field to identify common verb choices and adapt your writing and discussions accordingly.

By honing your verb usage skills, you will elevate your ability to communicate effectively in academic settings. This mastery will not only enhance your writing but also contribute to meaningful and impactful discussions within your academic community.

CHAPTER 20: Review & Practice: Verb Mastery Exercises

Verbs are the backbone of any sentence, providing the action and vitality that bring language to life. In this section, we've curated a series of exercises designed to enhance your mastery of verbs and elevate your communication skills.

Exercise 1:

Fill in the blank with the correct form of the *be* verb (am, is, are)

Example: My mother _____ at home.

Answer: My mother.....**is**....... at home.

They _____ happy.

She _____ on the phone.

My computer _____ broken.

I _____ sure.

Her name _____ Sarah.

My father and I _____ on vacation.

My friend Charlie _____ lost.

We _____ in the library.

My shoes _____ dirty.

My shoe _____ clean.

Answers

They ….. **are** …… happy.

She ….. **is** …… on the phone.

My computer .....**is**...... broken.

I ….. am…… sure.

Her name .....**is**..... Sarah.

My father and I ......**are**..... on vacation.

My friend Charlie .....**is**...... lost.

We .....**are**..... in the library.

My shoes .....**are**..... dirty.

My shoe .....**is**..... clean.

Exercise 2:

Use the words to create a Yes/No question using the "be" verb.

Example: (happy/you)

<u>Answer:</u> Are you happy?

- at home/ my brother
- sick/ they
- the computer/ expensive
- hot today/ it
- good/ the waves
- I/ in trouble
- late/ we
- your friends/ nice

Answers

- Is my brother at home?
- Are they sick?
- Is the computer expensive?
- Is it hot today?

- Are the waves good?
- Am I in trouble?
- Are we late?
- Are your friends nice?

Exercise 3:

Make questions using the following words and adding the correct form of the 'be' verb. Make sure you use the correct format:

[Wh word + be verb + subject + complement]

Example: (you from/ where)

Answer: Where are you from?

- (What/that)
- (Who/she)
- (Where/my pants)
- (When/you/at home)

- (Why /I /here)
- (How/ your cousins)
- (Why/ you/ on the phone)

Answers

- What is that?
- Who is she?
- Where are my pants?
- When are you at home?

- Why am I here?
- How are your cousins?
- Why are you on the phone?

Exercise 4:

Fill in the blank with the correct term (this, that, those, these)

Example: _____ is a great party. (You are at the party)

Answer: ....**This**........is a great party.

Can you see a girl over there with black pants and a blue shirt? _____ is my sister.

I want you to meet my friend. Susan, _____ is Sara. Sara, this is Susan.

_____ are my friends. This is Sara. This is Maria. This is Mike.

Can you see two big dogs across the street? _____ are my dogs.

Answers

Can you see a girl over there with black pants and a blue shirt? **.....That.....** is my sister.

I want you to meet my friend. Susan, **....this....** is Sara. Sara **.....this ....**is Susan.

.....These..... are my friends. This is Sara. This is Maria. This is Mike.
Can you see two big dogs across the street? **......Those.....** are my dogs.

Exercise 5:

Identify the verb in each sentence:
- She quickly ran to the store.
- The sun sets in the west.
- The cat slept on the cozy blanket.

Answers:

- Ran
- Sets
- Slept

Exercise 6:

Complete each sentence with the correct preposition following the verb.
- She apologized _____(her) mistake.
- They are interested _____(learning) new skills.

Answers:

- For
- In

Exercise 7:

Choose the appropriate modal verb to complete each sentence.
- You _____(can, must) finish the assignment by tomorrow.
- She _____(might, should) attend the meeting.

Answers:

- Must
- Should

Exercise 8:

Choose the appropriate options from the statements below:
_____along with me. (A. Read B. Reading C. Is reading)
Answer: A

He likes _____. (A. dancing B. dance)
Answer: A

You should _____ the floor. (A. scrubs B. scrub)
Answer: B

I ____ he was coming yesterday. (A. learned B. learnt C. was learning)
Answer: A

She _____ my assistance on her assignment. (A. request B. requested C. requested for)
Answer: B

We _____ his appearance in court last week. (A. demanded B. demanded for C. demand)
Answer: A

We _____ God. (A. depend B. depending on C. depend on)
Answer: C

BOOK 3: COMMON PHRASES FOR EVERYDAY USE

Have you ever found yourself in a conversation, grappling for the right words to express your thoughts or respond appropriately? Language, with its intricate web of expressions, is the key to effective communication, and mastering common phrases can significantly enhance your ability to navigate daily interactions. Welcome to "Common Phrases for Everyday Use," a comprehensive guide designed to empower you with the linguistic tools needed to navigate the intricacies of everyday communication.

In our fast-paced world, where connections are often forged through the exchange of words, the ability to use common phrases fluently is an invaluable skill. This book is a curated collection of phrases that cover a spectrum of situations, from casual conversations to professional settings, helping you articulate your ideas with confidence and clarity.

Whether you're a native English speaker looking to refine your expression or someone learning English as a second language, this book is crafted to cater to diverse linguistic needs. Each section is tailored to address specific contexts, offering you a reservoir of phrases that will enable you to engage in meaningful dialogue, build rapport, and express yourself with finesse.

Embark on this journey through "Common Phrases for Everyday Use," and discover the power of words to transform your daily interactions. As you delve into the pages ahead, you'll find a wealth of phrases that will not only broaden your vocabulary but also enrich your ability to connect with others on a deeper level. Get ready to unlock the door to effective communication and embrace the confidence that comes with mastering common phrases for everyday use.

CHAPTER 21: Greetings and Basic Interactions

Greetings serve as the initial notes in the symphony of social interaction, setting the tone for conversations to come. Whether formal or informal, these introductory moments play a significant role in establishing connections and fostering relationships.

Formal and Informal Greetings

In the vast landscape of English communication, understanding the nuances of formal and informal greetings is a crucial step toward becoming a confident speaker. This section will guide you through the art of salutations, providing you with the tools to navigate various social situations with ease.

Formal Greetings:
Formal greetings are used in professional and respectful settings, such as business meetings, interviews, or when addressing someone in a position of authority. Mastering these greetings is essential for creating a positive first impression.

Hello/Hi [Title + Last Name]:
Example: Hello, Mr. Johnson.
Use this in professional settings when addressing someone by their title and last name.

Good Morning/Afternoon/Evening [Title + Last Name]:
Example: Good evening, Professor Smith.
Employ these greetings based on the time of day, coupled with the person's title and last name.

How do you do?:
Example: How do you do, Mrs. Davis?
This is a formal greeting often used when meeting someone for the first time.

Nice to meet you:
Example: Nice to meet you, Dr. Anderson.
Express this when meeting someone new in a professional context.

Informal Greetings:
Informal greetings are employed in more casual, familiar situations, such as social gatherings or when conversing with friends and family. They allow for a more relaxed and friendly tone.

Hello/Hi [First Name]:
Example: Hi, Sarah!
Perfect for casual and informal settings, addressing someone by their first name.

Hey [First Name]:
Example: Hey, John!

A friendly and informal way to greet someone you know well.

What's up?:

Example: What's up, Alex?

A common and casual greeting among friends, asking about someone's well-being.

How's it going?:

Example: How's it going, Jessica?

An informal way to inquire about someone's current state or circumstances.

Vocabulary

Hello	Goodbye
How are you?	What is your name?
See you again	See you around
Take it easy	How's it going?
Are you ok?	Nice to meet you

Formal	Informal
Hello	Hi
Goodbye	See you around
How are you?	Take it easy
What is your name?	How's it going
Nice to meet you	Are you ok?
See you again	Bye bye
Pleased to meet you	Bye

Remember!

Friend – someone you know well.

Stranger – someone who you don't know

Colleague – someone you work with.

Acquaintance - Someone you don't know very well.

Sentence Structure

Question	Answer
Hello, how are you?	I'm fine thank you.
Hello, what is your name?	Hello, my name is Julian.
Nice to meet you. What is your name?	Nice to meet you too. My name is Sophie.
Hi, how's it going?	Good thanks, and you?
Hi, how are you?	I'm very well thank you, and you?

Person A	Person B
Nice to meet you.	Nice to meet you too.
See you again, goodbye.	Ok, goodbye.
Pleased to meet you.	Yes, you too.
Goodbye, see you around.	See you.
Hi!	Hi!
Goodbye, see you around.	See you.

By mastering the art of both formal and informal greetings, you'll be well-equipped to navigate the diverse social landscape of English communication. Remember, the key is to match the tone of your greeting with the context of the situation, ensuring that you leave a positive and lasting impression on those you interact with.

Making Small Talk

Small talk is a crucial skill in English communication. It helps you build connections, create a friendly atmosphere, and navigate social situations with ease. In this section, we'll explore the art of making small talk and provide you with practical tips to engage in light conversations effortlessly.

Small talk can cover a myriad of topics, ranging from the weather and current events to shared experiences or interests. It's an art that involves balancing between being engaging and not intruding into personal boundaries. Being attentive to cues and responding appropriately helps in steering the conversation and building rapport.
Effective small talk is not just about talking; it's about active listening. Paying attention to verbal and non-verbal cues allows individuals to connect on a deeper level, fostering a sense of understanding and mutual interest.

Remembering details from previous conversations, acknowledging shared experiences, and expressing genuine curiosity about the other person's thoughts and opinions contribute to the richness of small talk. It transforms seemingly inconsequential discussions into building blocks for stronger connections.

1. Start with Greetings:
Small talk often begins with a simple greeting. Whether you're meeting someone for the first time or catching up with a friend, a warm "hello" or "hi" sets the tone for a friendly exchange.

2. Weather Talk:
The weather is a classic topic for small talk. It's a safe and universal subject that everyone can relate to. You might say, "Beautiful weather we're having today, isn't it?" or "I heard it's going to rain later."

3. Common Ground:

Find common ground to connect with the other person. This could be a shared interest, a recent experience, or a mutual acquaintance. For example, "I heard you enjoy hiking. Do you have a favorite trail?" or "Did you catch that new movie everyone's talking about?"

4. Compliments:

Compliments are an excellent way to break the ice. Whether it's about someone's outfit, a recent achievement, or a skill they possess, genuine compliments create a positive atmosphere. "You look fantastic in that dress," or "Congratulations on your recent success at work!"

5. Open-ended Questions:

Ask open-ended questions to encourage the other person to share more about themselves. Instead of yes-or-no questions, try "What do you enjoy doing in your free time?" or "Tell me about your favorite vacation."

6. Active Listening:

Engage in active listening by nodding, making eye contact, and responding appropriately. Show genuine interest in the conversation, and don't hesitate to share your own thoughts and experiences.

7. Be Mindful of Cultural Differences:

Keep in mind cultural differences when engaging in small talk. Certain topics might be sensitive or inappropriate in some cultures, so be respectful and considerate.

Small talk is a great way to initiate conversations and build connections. Here are some common phrases you can use:

Greetings:

"Hi, how are you?"

"Hello, it's good to see you!"

"Hey there, what's new?"

Weather:

"Can you believe this weather?"

"Is it just me, or has it been really hot/cold lately?"

"Have you been enjoying the sunshine/rain?"

Weekend Plans:

"Any exciting plans for the weekend?"

"Doing anything fun over the weekend?"

"Got any special plans coming up?"

Work/Study:

"How's work/school going for you?"

"What do you do for a living/study?"

"Have you been busy at work/school?"

Hobbies and Interests:

"Do you have any hobbies you're passionate about?"

"Have you picked up any new interests lately?"

"What do you like to do in your free time?"

Movies/TV Shows:

"Seen any good movies or TV shows lately?"

"Do you have a favorite movie or TV series?"

"Any recommendations for something to watch?"

Travel:

"Have you been on any interesting trips recently?"

"If you could travel anywhere, where would you go?"

"Do you enjoy exploring new places?"

Food:

"Have you tried any new restaurants recently?"

"What's your favorite type of cuisine?"

"Do you enjoy cooking?"

Current Events:

"Did you hear about [current event]?"

"What are your thoughts on [current news topic]?"

"Anything interesting happening in the world lately?"

Compliments:

"That's a great [item of clothing]! Where did you get it?"

"You always have the best [accessory]! Where did you find it?"

"I love your [hairstyle/color]! It looks fantastic."

Remember, the key to successful small talk is to be genuine, listen actively, and show interest in the other person's responses.

Remember, small talk is about building connections and creating a comfortable environment. Practice these tips, and soon you'll find yourself navigating social situations with confidence and ease.

CHAPTER 22: Navigating Day-to-Day Activities

Discussing Routines and Hobbies

Learning a new language is not just about mastering grammar and vocabulary; it's also about expressing yourself in various contexts. In this chapter, we will explore the language needed to discuss your daily routines and hobbies. By the end of this section, you'll be able to engage in meaningful conversations about your daily life and interests.

1. Daily Routines:

Let's start by discussing your daily routine. Being able to describe your typical day is crucial in building connections and sharing experiences. Here are some common phrases and expressions to help you talk about your daily activities:

- I usually wake up at...
- After getting up, I...
- My morning routine includes...
- In the afternoon, I tend to...
- Evenings are usually dedicated to...
- Before going to bed, I...

Feel free to personalize these phrases based on your own schedule. Practice expressing your daily routine with a partner or in front of a mirror to build confidence in using these expressions naturally.

2. Hobbies and Interests:

Now, let's move on to discussing hobbies and interests. Being able to share what you enjoy doing during your leisure time helps create connections and find common ground with others. Here are some phrases to help you talk about your hobbies:
One of my favorite hobbies is...

- I really enjoy...
- During the weekends, I like to...
- In my free time, I often...
- I'm passionate about...
- A hobby I picked up recently is...

As with daily routines, feel free to tailor these expressions to match your own interests. Engage in conversations with classmates, language partners, or native speakers to practice discussing hobbies and discovering shared interests.

3. Combining Routines and Hobbies:

To make your conversations more dynamic, try combining discussions about routines and hobbies. For example:
"On weekdays, I usually wake up early and go for a run. Running is one of my favorite hobbies, and it helps me start the day with energy."
This type of integrated conversation not only showcases your language skills but also provides a holistic view of your lifestyle.

Remember, the key to mastering these topics is consistent practice. Engage in conversations, write journal entries, and challenge yourself to use these expressions in various contexts. The more you practice, the more confident and proficient you'll become in discussing your routines and hobbies in English.

Describing Feelings and Opinions

Understanding how to express your feelings and opinions is crucial when learning a new language. In this section, we will explore vocabulary and phrases that will help you articulate your thoughts in English. Being able to convey your emotions and viewpoints not only enhances your language skills but also allows you to connect more effectively with others.

1. Emotions Vocabulary:
Let's start by familiarizing ourselves with common emotions. Learning how to accurately describe what you're feeling is essential for effective communication. Here are some words to help you express your emotions:

- Happy: delighted, content, joyful
- Sad: upset, downhearted, melancholic
- Angry: furious, irritated, enraged
- Surprised: astonished, amazed, shocked
- Excited: thrilled, eager, enthusiastic
- Afraid: scared, frightened, anxious

2. Opinion Phrases:
Expressing your opinions is an integral part of communication. Whether you're discussing a movie, expressing preferences, or sharing your thoughts on a topic, having a variety of phrases at your disposal is key. Here are some phrases to help you convey your opinions effectively:

- In my opinion: This is a polite way to share what you think.
- I believe that: Use this when you want to express a belief or conviction.
- From my perspective: This phrase adds a personal touch to your opinion.
- It seems to me that: A great way to introduce a subjective viewpoint.
- I'm of the opinion that: This is a formal way to express your stance.
- As far as I'm concerned: Use this to emphasize your personal viewpoint.

3. Describing Intensity:

Sometimes, it's not just about expressing an emotion or opinion but conveying the intensity of it. Let's look at some phrases that help you express the strength of your feelings:

- I'm absolutely thrilled about...
- I strongly believe that...
- I'm really passionate about...

- I'm not particularly fond of...
- I'm somewhat indifferent to...
- I'm quite excited about...

To reinforce your understanding, engage in conversation or written exercises using the emotions vocabulary and opinion phrases provided. Discuss your feelings about various topics or express your opinions on different matters. This practice will help you become more comfortable using these expressions in real-life situations. Remember, the key to mastering feelings and opinions is practice. The more you engage with the language, the more natural and confident you will become in expressing yourself.

CHAPTER 23: Travel and Tourism Phrases

At the Airport and Public Transport

At the Airport

Airports can be bustling hubs of activity, and it's essential to feel comfortable navigating them, especially if you're traveling to an English-speaking country. Let's equip you with the right vocabulary and phrases to make your airport experience smoother.

1. Checking In:

Phrases:

- "I'd like to check in, please."
- "Do I need to show my ID and ticket?"
- "Is there a weight limit for my luggage?"

2. Security Check:

Vocabulary:

- Boarding pass
- Conveyor belt
- Metal detector

Phrases:

- "Where do I place my belongings for screening?"
- "Do I need to remove my shoes?"

3. Boarding the Plane:

Phrases:

- "When is the boarding time?"
- "Which gate is my flight departing from?"
- "May I see your boarding pass, please?"

4. In the Airplane:

Vocabulary:

- Overhead compartment
- Aisle seat
- Window seat

Phrases:

- "Excuse me, is this seat taken?"
- "Can I have a blanket, please?"

Public Transport Adventures

Once you've landed, public transportation will likely become a part of your journey. Whether it's buses, trains, or taxis, let's prepare you for these conversations.

1. Taking a Taxi:

Phrases:

- "I need a taxi to [your destination]."
- "How much is the fare to the city center?"
- "Can you please take me to the nearest hotel?"

2. Using Public Buses:

Vocabulary:

- Bus stop
- Fare
- Timetable

Phrases:

- "Which bus goes to [your destination]?"
- "How often do the buses run?"
- "Where can I buy a bus ticket?"

3. Navigating Trains:

Phrases:

- "Is this the right platform for the [train number]?"
- "How long is the journey to [your destination]?"
- "Are there any delays on this route?"

4. Asking for Directions:

Phrases:

- "Excuse me, could you help me find [your destination]?"
- "Is it within walking distance?"
- "Which way is the [landmark] from here?"

By mastering these airport and public transport conversations, you'll enhance your ability to communicate effectively during your travels. Practice these phrases, and soon you'll be navigating English-speaking airports and public transport systems with ease.

Hotel Bookings and Sightseeing

As you embark on your journey to become proficient in English, mastering conversations related to hotel bookings is essential. This section aims to equip you with the language skills needed to seamlessly reserve accommodation and navigate sightseeing plans during your travels.

Practice sharing necessary details like your name, the number of guests, and any specific preferences or requirements you may have. Politeness goes a long way. Master polite requests like "Could you please...?" or "I would appreciate it if..." Expressing gratitude is important. Practice saying "Thank you" and learn variations like "Thanks a lot" or "I'm grateful for your help." Learn to apologize if there are any inconveniences or misunderstandings during your interactions.

Here are some phrases you can use for hotel bookings and sightseeing:

Making a Reservation:
- "I would like to make a reservation for [number of nights] nights."
- "Can I book a room for [dates]?"
- "I'd like to reserve a [single/double] room, please."

Inquiring about Availability:
- "Do you have any rooms available for [dates]?"
- "What is your availability for the upcoming weekend?"
- "Are there any rooms left for tonight?"

Asking about Room Types:
- "Could you tell me about the different room types available?"
- "What are the amenities included in the [standard/deluxe/suite] room?"
- "Do you have any rooms with a [view/balcony]?"

Confirmation and Payment:
- "Can you confirm my reservation?"
- "What is your cancellation policy?"
- "What forms of payment do you accept?"

Special Requests:
- "I have a special request; can I have [extra bed/crib] in the room?"
- "Is it possible to have a room on a higher floor?"
- "I have dietary restrictions; can you accommodate them during breakfast?"

Sightseeing:
Asking for Recommendations:
"Could you recommend some must-see attractions in the area?"
"What are the top tourist spots around here?"
"Are there any hidden gems or local favorites you would suggest?"

Inquiring about Tours:
"Do you offer guided tours of the city?"
"Are there any day trips or excursions available?"
"Can you provide information on the historical/cultural tours?"

Transportation:
- "How can I get to [tourist attraction] from the hotel?"
- "Are there public transportation options nearby?"

- "Do you provide shuttle services to popular landmarks?"

Tickets and Admission:

- "Where can I purchase tickets for [museum/park]?"
- "Is it advisable to buy tickets in advance for popular attractions?"
- "What is the entrance fee for [landmark]?"

Local Etiquette:

- "Are there any cultural customs I should be aware of while sightseeing?"
- "Are there specific dress codes for certain attractions?"
- "Can you provide a map of the local area with key attractions marked?"

In mastering hotel bookings and sightseeing conversations, you not only enhance your language skills but also gain the confidence to navigate travel experiences with ease. Remember, practice makes perfect, so don't hesitate to immerse yourself in real-life situations whenever possible.

CHAPTER 24: Dining and Food

Ordering at Restaurants and Cafés

In this section, we will delve into essential phrases and expressions that will empower you to confidently order food and beverages at restaurants and cafés. Effective communication in these settings is not just about expressing your preferences, but also understanding the questions and prompts from the staff. Let's equip you with the language skills needed for a seamless dining experience.

Ordering at restaurants and cafes involves using polite and clear language to communicate your preferences. Here's a sequence of phrases that you might find helpful:

Greetings:

- "Hello" or "Hi" to acknowledge the staff.

Ask for a Table:

- "Do you have a table available?"
- "May I have a table for [number] people, please?"

Ordering Drinks:

- "Could I start with a [beverage]?"
- "I'll have a [name of the drink], please."
- "May I get a glass of water, please?"

Ordering Food:

- "For starters, I would like [appetizer]."
- "I'll have the [name of the dish] for the main course."
- "Could I have [special dish], please?"
- "Is [dish] spicy/mild? I prefer [your preference]."

Customizing Your Order:

- "Can I get that without [ingredient]?"
- "Could you make it [cooked level], please?"
- "I'd like [side dish] instead of [default side]."

Confirming the Order:

- "So, just to confirm, I ordered [repeat your order], right?"
- "Did I miss anything in my order?"

Asking Questions:

- "What do you recommend?"
- "Could you tell me more about [dish]?"
- "Are there any vegetarian/vegan options?"

Special Requests:

- "Could I have the dressing/sauce on the side?"
- "Is it possible to make it a bit [more/less] [specific request]?"

Dessert or Coffee:
- "I'm interested in the [dessert name], please."
- "Can I get a [type of coffee] after the meal?"

Requesting the Bill:
- "May we have the bill, please?"
- "Could you bring us the check when you get a chance?"

Expressing Gratitude:
- "Thank you so much!"
- "I appreciate your help."

Always thank the staff for their service. A simple "Thank you" or "Thanks a lot" goes a long way.

By mastering these ordering conversations, you'll not only enjoy your dining experiences but also build confidence in your English communication skills. Practice these phrases, and soon, ordering at restaurants and cafés will become second nature to you.

Talking About Food Preferences

In this section, we will delve into the delightful world of discussing food preferences in English. Food is not only a necessity but also a universal language of joy. Being able to express your likes and dislikes about food can make your dining experiences more enjoyable and help you connect with others. Let's explore some key phrases and expressions to master this essential aspect of communication.

1. Expressing Likes:
- I love [food]. It's my absolute favorite.
- [Food] is delicious. I can't get enough of it.
- I really enjoy [food]. It's fantastic.

2. Describing Dislikes:
- I'm not a fan of [food]. It's just not my thing.
- [Food] is not to my taste. I find it a bit too [spicy/sweet/salty].
- I can't stand [food]. I prefer something else.

3. Asking for Recommendations:
- Can you recommend any good [cuisine/restaurant] around here?
- What's your favorite [dish]? I'm looking to try something new.
- Any suggestions on where I can find delicious [food]?

4. Exploring Dietary Preferences:
- I'm vegetarian/vegan. Do you have any options for me?
- I have allergies to [ingredient]. Is there anything on the menu without it?
- I'm trying to eat healthier. Any light or low-fat options?

5. Polite Expressions:
- Thank you, this is wonderful!

- I appreciate your recommendation.
- I'm not a big fan, but it's very well-prepared.

6. Talking about Cooking:

- I enjoy cooking [type of cuisine].
- My specialty is [dish]. Would you like to try it sometime?
- I'm still learning to cook. Any easy recipes you recommend?

By mastering these phrases, you'll be well-equipped to navigate conversations about food preferences with confidence. Don't be afraid to experiment with new tastes and flavors. Food is a fantastic way to connect with people and explore different cultures.

CHAPTER 25: Shopping and Transactions

Clothing and Electronics

Learning English involves mastering conversations about various everyday topics. In this section, we will focus on two essential aspects of daily life: clothing and electronics. These topics are not only integral to our day-to-day experiences but also provide an excellent opportunity to expand your English vocabulary and communication skills.

Clothing Conversations:
Greetings at a Clothing Store:
- When entering a clothing store, a simple greeting could be: "Hello! How may I help you today?"
- Common responses: "I'm just browsing, thank you," or "I'm looking for [specific item]."

Asking for Assistance:
- Phrases like "Could you help me find the fitting room?" or "Where are the women's/men's/kids' section?" are handy.
- Describing what you're looking for: "I'm searching for a formal dress for a special occasion."

In the Fitting Room:
- Expressing opinions: "I like this one, but do you have it in a different color?"
- Seeking assistance with sizes: "Could I try this in a smaller/bigger size, please?"

Making a Purchase:
- Asking about discounts: "Are there any sales or discounts happening?"
- Making a decision: "I'll take this one, please. Do you accept credit cards?"

Electronics Conversations:
At an Electronics Store:
- Opening the conversation: "Hello, I'm looking for a [specific electronic device]. Can you help me find it?"
- Asking for recommendations: "What's the latest model of [device]?"

Inquiring about Features:
- "Can you tell me more about the features of this product?"
- Comparing options: "How does this one differ from the other models?"

Technical Assistance:
- Describing an issue: "My [device] isn't working properly. Can you help me troubleshoot?"
- Seeking help with setup: "I'm having trouble setting up my [device]. Could you guide me through it?"

Making a Purchase:

- Confirming details: "Does the price include a warranty?"
- Payment options: "Do you accept cash or card? Is there an installment plan available?"

Remember to practice these phrases and engage in role-play scenarios to boost your confidence in using them. Whether you're shopping for a new wardrobe or exploring the latest electronics, these conversations will prove invaluable in your English language journey.

Bargaining and Making Payments

Here are some phrases you can use for bargaining and making payments:

Bargaining:

Initiating the Bargain:
- "Can we discuss the price a bit?"
- "I was wondering if there's any flexibility in the price."
- "Is there room for negotiation on this?"

Expressing Interest:
- "I really like this, but I was hoping for a better price."
- "If we can find a middle ground on the price, I'm ready to make a deal."
- "I'm interested in buying, but the budget is a bit tight. Any chance for a discount?"

Comparing Prices:
- "I've seen similar items priced lower elsewhere. Can you match that?"
- "I'm exploring other options; can you offer a more competitive price?"

Bundling:
- "If I purchase this along with [another item], could we work out a better deal?"
- "What if I buy in bulk? Is there a discount for larger quantities?"

Remaining Polite:
- "I really like your product, but I need to stay within a certain budget. Can you help?"
- "I appreciate your time. Is there any way we can find a price that works for both of us?"

Making Payments:

Confirming the Amount:

"Just to confirm, the total amount is [amount], correct?"

"Could you please provide a breakdown of the charges before I proceed?"

Payment Method:

"What payment methods do you accept?"

"Is credit card the preferred method, or do you accept other forms of payment?"

Requesting a Receipt:

- "Can I get a receipt for this transaction, please?"
- "Is it possible to receive an electronic receipt via email?"

Payment Plan:

- "If the total amount is a bit high, do you offer any payment plans?"
- "I'm interested in a payment installment option. Is that available?"

Expressing Appreciation:

- "Thank you for your assistance. I'm ready to make the payment now."
- "I appreciate your help in making this transaction smooth."

Remember to adapt these phrases based on the specific context and cultural norms. Being polite and respectful in your communication will generally lead to more positive outcomes in both bargaining and making payments.

CHAPTER 26: Medical and Emergency Situations

Visiting the Doctor or Hospital

1. Making an Appointment:

Dialogue: At the Reception

- Patient: Hello, I would like to schedule an appointment with Dr. Smith, please.
- Receptionist: Sure, could you please provide your name and date of birth?
- Patient: My name is Sarah Johnson, and my date of birth is March 15, 1985.
- Receptionist: Thank you, Sarah. Dr. Smith has availability on Monday at 2:00 PM. Does that work for you?
- Patient: Yes, that's fine. Thank you.

2. Describing Symptoms:

Dialogue: Speaking to the Nurse

- Nurse: Good afternoon, Sarah. What seems to be the issue today?
- Patient: Hi, I've been experiencing a persistent headache and a sore throat for the past few days.
- Nurse: I see. Are you also having any fever or difficulty breathing?
- Patient: No fever, but I do feel a bit congested.
- Nurse: Thank you for letting me know. Dr. Smith will be with you shortly.

3. Doctor-Patient Consultation:

Dialogue: Talking to the Doctor

- Dr. Smith: Hello, Sarah. How can I help you today?
- Patient: Hi, Dr. Smith. I've had this headache and sore throat, and I feel congested.
- Dr. Smith: I see. Let me check your vitals and then we'll discuss your symptoms in more detail.
  After examination
- Dr. Smith: It seems like you might have a mild cold. I'll prescribe some medication to help alleviate your symptoms. Make sure to get plenty of rest and stay hydrated.

4. Understanding Medical Instructions:

Dialogue: Pharmacy Interaction

- Pharmacist: Good afternoon, Sarah. Here are the medications prescribed by Dr. Smith. Take one tablet with meals, and this cough syrup should be taken before bedtime.
- Patient: Thank you. Should I avoid anything while taking these?
- Pharmacist: It's best to avoid alcohol while on these medications. If you experience any unusual side effects, consult your doctor.

Seeking Help in Urgent Situations

In our daily lives, there may be times when we find ourselves in urgent situations that require quick and effective communication. Learning how to seek help in such situations is a crucial aspect of mastering the English language. In this section, we will explore common phrases and expressions that can be used when seeking assistance in urgent scenarios.

1. Emergency Vocabulary:
- Help! - A universal cry for immediate assistance.
- Call 911 (or emergency services): In English-speaking countries, this is the standard emergency number. Be familiar with the equivalent in your region.

2. Describing the Situation:
- I need help quickly. There's an emergency.
- There's been an accident. Can you call for help?

3. Providing Important Information:
- Give your location: "I am at [specific location]."
- Describe the situation: "There's a fire/burglary/car accident."

4. Medical Emergencies:
- I need a doctor/ambulance.
- Someone has collapsed. We need medical assistance.

5. Asking for Assistance from Bystanders:
- Excuse me, can you help me?
- Please call for help. It's an emergency.

6. Expressing Urgency:
- It's urgent! We need immediate assistance.
- Quick, please! Time is of the essence.

7. Gratitude and Appreciation:
- Thank you for your help. I appreciate it.
- Your quick response means a lot.

Remember, mastering the language in urgent situations is not only about the words you use but also about your tone and clarity. Practice these phrases regularly to build confidence and ensure that you can navigate emergency situations with ease.

CHAPTER 27: Social Etiquette and Cultural Phrases

Invitations and Celebrations

Making Invitations:

1. Casual Invitations:

Casual invitations are often used among friends and family. Keep the tone friendly and informal.

Example:

Hey, would you like to grab a coffee this weekend?

We're having a small get-together at our place on Friday. Are you free to join?

2. Formal Invitations:

Formal invitations are suitable for official events or gatherings. Use polite language and include details about the event.

Example:

You are cordially invited to attend the annual company dinner on Saturday, the 22nd of May, at 7:00 PM.

We request the pleasure of your company at the wedding ceremony of [Name] and [Name] on the 10th of June.

Responding to Invitations:

1. Accepting Invitations:

When accepting an invitation, express gratitude and confirm your attendance.

Example:

Thank you for the invitation! I'd love to come.

I appreciate the invite. I'll be there for sure.

2. Declining Invitations:

If you can't attend, be polite and offer a brief explanation.

Example:

I'm sorry, but I have a prior commitment that day.

Thanks for inviting me, but I won't be able to make it.

Celebrating Special Occasions:

1. Birthday Wishes:

Offering birthday wishes is a common celebration. Use warm and sincere language.

Example:

Wishing you a fantastic birthday filled with joy and laughter!

May this year bring you success and happiness. Happy Birthday!

2. Congratulations:

Congratulating someone on an achievement or milestone is a positive and uplifting gesture.

Example:

Congratulations on your promotion! You truly deserve it.

Wishing you both a lifetime of love and happiness. Congratulations on your wedding!

Apologizing and Expressing Gratitude

In everyday communication, expressing apologies and gratitude are essential social skills. Whether you find yourself in a situation where you need to apologize for a mistake or express gratitude for a kind gesture, mastering these conversations will greatly enhance your ability to connect with others. In this section, we'll explore common scenarios and phrases for both apologizing and expressing gratitude.

1. Apologizing Conversations:

Scenario 1: Apologizing for Being Late

A: I'm sorry I'm late.

B: No problem. What happened?

A: There was unexpected traffic on the way here.

Scenario 2: Apologizing for a Mistake at Work

A: I want to apologize for the error in the report.

B: It's okay. Let's work together to fix it.

A: I appreciate your understanding.

Scenario 3: Apologizing for Canceling Plans

A: I'm really sorry, but I have to cancel our plans for tonight.

B: That's okay. Is everything alright?

A: I had a family emergency, and I need to be there.

2. Expressing Gratitude Conversations:

Scenario 1: Thanking Someone for Help

A: Thank you so much for helping me with the moving.

B: It was my pleasure. Let me know if you need anything else.

A: I really appreciate it.

Scenario 2: Expressing Gratitude for a Gift

A: This gift is amazing. Thank you!

B: I'm glad you like it. You deserve it.

A: It means a lot to me.

Scenario 3: Showing Appreciation at Work

A: I wanted to express my gratitude for your guidance on the project.

B: It's a team effort, and you contributed a lot.

A: Thank you for your support.

By practicing these apologizing and expressing gratitude conversations, you'll become more comfortable navigating social situations. Remember, sincerity and genuine communication go a long way in building positive relationships.

CHAPTER 28: Expressions in Love and Relationships

Romantic Phrases and Compliments

Learning to express romantic feelings and compliments is an essential part of mastering English for adults. Whether you're in a relationship or trying to impress someone special, the right words can make all the difference. In this section, we'll explore various romantic phrases and compliments that you can use in different situations.

1. Expressing Affection:

- "I adore you."
- "You mean the world to me."
- "You are the love of my life."

2. Complimenting Appearance:

- "You look stunning today."
- "Your smile lights up the room."
- "I can't take my eyes off you."

3. Praising Personality:

- "I love your sense of humor."
- "You're so kind and caring."
- "Your intelligence is incredibly attractive."

4. Romantic Gestures:

- "I appreciate the little things you do for me."
- "You make every moment special."
- "Being with you is like a dream come true."

5. Expressing Love:

- "I love you more and more each day."
- "You complete me."
- "My heart belongs to you."

6. Planning Romantic Dates:

- "How about a romantic dinner this weekend?"
- "I'd love to take you out for a special evening."
- "Let's create beautiful memories together."

7. Apologizing and Reassuring:

- "I'm sorry if I upset you; you mean everything to me."
- "I didn't mean to hurt your feelings."
- "I value our relationship, and I'll make it right."

8. Surprise and Excitement:

- "I have a surprise for you!"
- "I can't wait to see the look on your face."
- "You're going to love what I have planned."

Remember, the key to using these phrases is sincerity. Speak from the heart, and your words will carry genuine meaning. Practice incorporating these expressions into your daily conversations to become more comfortable with expressing romantic feelings in English.

Discussing Relationship Issues

In this section, we will delve into conversations that revolve around relationship issues, an essential aspect of adult life. Effective communication in relationships is crucial for building strong connections and resolving conflicts. Learning to express oneself and understanding your partner's perspective can lead to healthier, more fulfilling relationships.

1. Expressing Feelings:

Learning to articulate your emotions is fundamental in any relationship. Whether you're expressing joy, frustration, or concern, it's important to use words that convey your feelings accurately. Practice using phrases such as:

- I feel... when... because...
- It makes me happy/sad/angry when...
- I appreciate it when you...

2. Active Listening:

Communication is a two-way street. Being an active listener is as crucial as expressing yourself. Encourage your partner to share their thoughts and feelings by using phrases like:

- I understand how you feel.
- Tell me more about your perspective.
- I'm here for you.

3. Conflict Resolution:

Every relationship encounters challenges. Learning to navigate through conflicts is key to maintaining a healthy connection. Practice using phrases that promote understanding and compromise:

- Let's talk about what happened.
- I see where you're coming from, but I feel...
- How can we find a solution together?

4. Apologizing and Forgiving:

Admitting mistakes and forgiving are essential skills for maintaining harmony in relationships. Explore phrases that convey sincerity and openness:

- I'm sorry for...
- I didn't mean to hurt you.
- Can we move forward and learn from this?

5. Discussing Future Plans:

Relationships often involve planning for the future. Whether it's short-term goals or long-term aspirations, practice using phrases like:

- I envision our future together as...
- What are your goals for the next few years?
- How can we work towards our shared dreams?

Remember, the key to successful communication in relationships is a combination of expressing yourself, actively listening, and finding common ground. Use these phrases as a foundation to build strong, open, and fulfilling connections with those you care about.

CHAPTER 29: English in the Digital Age

Technology is constantly changing and at an increasingly fast pace. Historically, language has evolved along with new developments in technology, and it's important to understand this relationship. Language is always changing, and terminology and slang from even fifty years ago sound ancient now. You'd need to watch an old black-and-white film to hear people greet one other with How are you doing? In this section, we'll look at the evolution of English, how text messaging has changed our language, and how to use English in the modern world.

Throughout history, new technology have led to the development of new and adaptable languages. Today, when you want to get some information about a topic, you google it. You text your sister and e-mail your customers during work, and after work, you might tweet or snap your buddies.

Technology also brings us new meanings by adapting old words. **Friend** is now a verb: You **friend** and **unfriend** people on social media. A **cloud** is a place for online data storage. A **cookie** went from a sweet baked snack to a piece of data on your computer. The noun feed may still refer to animal food on farms, but in most cases, it refers to the thread of information that is updated on your social network. A tag has evolved from a sticker on bread to a technique to identify someone in a photograph.

Technology has had an impact on more than only language. According to an Oxford University Press study published in 2015, the word hashtag and its symbol, #, have become a word used offline by youngsters under the age of thirteen. "Hashtag" was first used on Twitter to signify relevant keywords, but it has since become popular among people of all ages in ordinary written language for "dramatic effect."
New ideas for words and grammar can even stem from memes, like "doing me a frighten," a meme in the voice of a startled dog in a type of "doggolingo" Internet language used in dog memes. Technically, the grammar of this sentence is incorrect—but in the language of a frightened dog friend, it's just right.

Lastly, it's hard to miss the text initialisms, or abbreviations, that have come into existence, such as LOL (laughing out loud), NVM (never mind), LMK (let me know), and IDK (I don't know). Language and grammar depend on the type of technology being used, but we can be certain that they will continue to change over time as technology and online communities evolve and influence one another.
Let's Talk about Texting

Text messaging, or **texting**, has had a tremendous impact on language. Texting is casual, conversational, and brief. In fact, texting is more like speaking than writing. That's because in many cases, people communicate via texting in real time, so what they type is usually similar to what they would say in person.

Texting and instant messaging have boosted the popularity of initialisms and emoticons. Popular initialisms—acronyms like BRB (be right back), BTW (by the way), and OFC (of course)—made it easier to express ourselves on pre-smartphone cell phones, and symbols through typing became popular to send messages, such as:) for a smile, ;) for a wink, and:* for a kiss. As mobile communication improved, little graphics known as emojis replaced those symbols.

The language of texting is likewise developing its own grammar. According to John McWhorter's 2013 TED Talk, LOL (laughing out loud) is being utilized as a discourse marker in texting, similar to uh-huh, well, and you know. For example:

Omar: Do you wanna grab dinner after work?

Rick: LOL I'm working until 10 p.m.

Rick isn't laughing about working until ten (although maybe he's laughing a sad, tired laugh at 9:30 p.m.). He's using LOL with the meaning of **ah**, **well**, or **no can do**. This type of usage of LOL has even made its way back into spoken English!

Adapting to Digital Communication

The emergence of digital communication has created both benefits and challenges. Many people nowadays prefer to text or message rather than speak in person or on the phone. Social media has introduced new opportunities to communicate with people via images, videos, and text. The digital world has given us the ability to socialize and collaborate with others regardless of our physical location, which has affected how we use and think about language.

One area in which we still need to curb this modern communication style is in business situations. While short, ungrammatical phrases are perfectly acceptable in a text, they won't be well received in most business situations. This, of course, varies depending on the industry, but often, the language used is expected to be more traditionally, formally written—especially when communicating with clients. TY (thank you) is not appropriate to write when thanking a customer for a hundred-thousand-dollar order—in fact, it would be considered an insult. In general, digital communication in the workplace is limited to words and does not include emojis or time-saving acronyms.

The capacity to conduct business in a global context means that we communicate with people from all over the world more than ever before. While English is the international business language, not everyone understands its intricacies. Self-awareness of your language can help you communicate more successfully, especially if you work in an international setting. Avoid using idioms and informal language that your global colleagues may not understand, regardless of the language.

Students and English learners often tell me they hear and see a lot of different kinds of English these days, and some of what they run into doesn't seem to follow a rule. They're right. In fact, there are a lot of times you actually don't need any of these rules when you communicate.

Mia: Hey!
Caden: What's up?
Mia: Hungry?
Caden: LOL totally
Mia: Pizza?
Caden: Awesome
Mia: Cool. Let's go

You may have such chats (verbal or text) on a regular basis or know someone who does. This puts us in context. Context—the situation you're in—is one of the most fundamental notions and guiding principles in any language. It is acceptable to bend or even break the rules, depending on the circumstances. When applying for a job or requesting a professor for a deadline extension, you'll pay much more attention to the regulations than when responding to a casual offer from your friend. In general, the more formal the occasion, the more vocabulary and language you'll employ. For example:

- Thank you so much for studying here with me. I really appreciate it.
- Thanks for studying here with me. I appreciate it.
- Thanks for studying here. I appreciate it.
- Thanks for studying.
- Thanks a lot.
- Keep Writing

Online Communication and Social Media

In today's digital age, online communication and social media play a significant role in connecting people around the world. Whether you're a beginner or an advanced learner, understanding how to navigate these platforms can enhance your English language skills and broaden your cultural awareness.

This section will guide you through the basics of online communication and help you engage in meaningful conversations on social media.

Online communication includes various platforms like email, messaging apps, and video calls. These tools provide instant communication, allowing you to connect with friends, family, and colleagues globally. Pay attention to common phrases used in emails and messaging to effectively express yourself.

Social Media Vocabulary:

Social media platforms such as Facebook, Twitter, and Instagram have their unique vocabulary. Learn terms like "post," "like," "comment," and "share." Understanding these words will enable you to navigate these platforms confidently.

Constructing Social Media Posts:

Practice creating engaging social media posts. Learn how to express your thoughts, share experiences, and ask questions. This will not only improve your writing skills but also enhance your ability to connect with others online.

Effective Communication on Social Media:

Explore the etiquettes of online communication. Understand the tone of different platforms and tailor your messages accordingly. Learn to express agreement, disagreement, and gratitude in a polite and concise manner.

Common Abbreviations and Acronyms:

Social media often uses abbreviations and acronyms for brevity. Familiarize yourself with common ones like LOL (laugh out loud), BRB (be right back), and BTW (by the way). This knowledge will help you understand and respond to messages more efficiently.

Emojis and Emoticons:

Emojis and emoticons add a personal touch to online communication. Learn their meanings and when it's appropriate to use them. Understanding the nuances of these symbols will help you convey emotions effectively.

Joining Online Communities:

Explore online communities related to your interests. Participate in discussions, share your thoughts, and engage with others. This immersive experience will expose you to diverse language styles and cultural expressions.

Handling Disagreements:

Learn how to navigate disagreements respectfully. Online platforms can sometimes lead to misunderstandings.

Practice expressing your opinions in a diplomatic manner, and be open to different perspectives.

By mastering online communication and social media conversations, you'll not only enhance your English skills but also become a more effective communicator in today's interconnected world. Embrace the opportunities these platforms offer to practice, learn, and connect with people from various backgrounds.

Understanding Internet Slang

In today's digital age, communication has evolved beyond traditional language norms, and the internet plays a significant role in shaping how we interact. Internet slang, also known as "netspeak" or "cyber language," has become a vital aspect of online conversations. As an adult beginner learning English, it's important to familiarize yourself with common internet slang to better navigate the virtual world and engage in meaningful online dialogues.

Internet slang consists of abbreviations, acronyms, and informal expressions used primarily in online communication. These shortcuts and informal terms are employed to convey messages quickly and efficiently. While they may seem cryptic at first, understanding internet slang can greatly enhance your ability to participate in online discussions and connect with others on social media platforms.

Common Internet Slang Terms

- LOL - Laugh Out Loud: Used to indicate that something is funny. For example, "That joke was hilarious, LOL!"
- BRB - Be Right Back: Signifying a temporary absence from the conversation. "I'll BRB, just grabbing a snack."
- OMG - Oh My God: Expressing surprise or disbelief. "OMG, I can't believe you did that!"
- ICYMI - In Case You Missed It: Used when sharing information that someone might have missed. "ICYMI, we're meeting at 3 PM tomorrow."
- IMO/IMHO - In My Opinion/In My Humble Opinion: Inserting a personal viewpoint into the conversation. "IMHO, the movie was fantastic."
- TMI - Too Much Information: Used to convey that someone has shared more details than necessary. "TMI, I don't need to know all the specifics."

Tips for Understanding Internet Slang

Context Matters: Pay attention to the context of the conversation. Understanding the overall discussion can help you interpret the meaning of internet slang terms.

Observe and Learn: Spend time observing how internet slang is used in various online communities. This will help you become familiar with commonly used expressions.

Ask for Clarification: Don't hesitate to ask for clarification if you come across an unfamiliar term. Online communities are often welcoming and willing to help newcomers.

CHAPTER 30: Review & Practice: Phrase Mastery Exercises

Learning English is not just about mastering individual words; it's also about becoming proficient in using phrases and expressions that are commonly used in everyday conversations. In this section, we will focus on honing your ability to use and understand essential English phrases.

Exercise 1:

Everyday Expressions
Objective: Familiarize yourself with common phrases used in daily conversations.
Greetings and Farewells:
Practice using greetings like "Hello," "Hi," and "How are you?"
Experiment with different ways to say goodbye, such as "Goodbye," "See you later," or "Take care."
Polite Requests:
Learn phrases for making polite requests, like "Could you please...?" or "Would you mind...?"
Create your own sentences using these polite request forms.

Exercise 2:

Phrasal Verbs
Objective: Understand and use phrasal verbs in context.
Identify the Phrasal Verb:
Given a sentence, identify the phrasal verb used and its meaning.
Example: "She put off the meeting." (Phrasal Verb: put off, Meaning: postpone)
Create Sentences:
Form sentences using common phrasal verbs. For instance, "I ran into an old friend yesterday." (Phrasal Verb: run into, Meaning: unexpectedly meet)

Exercise 3:

Expressing Opinions
Objective: Develop the ability to express opinions clearly.
Discussing Likes and Dislikes:
Practice using phrases like "I really enjoy," "I don't like," or "I prefer."
Share your preferences with a study partner and ask for theirs.
Giving Reasons:
Strengthen your ability to provide reasons for your opinions.
Example: "I prefer reading because it helps me relax, and I learn new things."

Exercise 4:

Common Questions and Responses
Objective: Improve your question-forming and responding skills.
Ask and Answer:
Practice asking common questions like "What do you do?" or "How was your day?"
Respond appropriately and extend the conversation.
Role Play:
Engage in role-play scenarios where you ask and answer questions in different contexts (e.g., at a restaurant, during a job interview).

Exercise 5:

Slang and Informal Expressions
Objective: Familiarize yourself with informal language used in casual conversations.
Learn Slang Terms:
Explore common slang expressions and understand their meanings.
Use them in sentences to get a feel for how they are naturally employed.
Casual Conversations:
Practice having casual conversations using the slang and informal expressions learned.

Exercise 6:

Simulate hotel booking and sightseeing scenarios with a language partner or use online resources that provide interactive language practice.

Exercise 7:

Make a list of five new words or meanings for words (not discussed in this section) that have come into existence because of technology. Then use those words in a sentence, keeping in mind their new definitions and contexts.

BOOK 4: WORKBOOK TO SPEAK ENGLISH IN NO TIME

CHAPTER 31: Basic Vocabulary Building

Have you ever found yourself yearning to effortlessly communicate in English, to seamlessly express your thoughts and ideas with confidence? Welcome to the "Workbook to Speak English in No Time." This comprehensive guide is designed to transform your language learning journey into an exciting and efficient adventure.

In a world where English has become the global language of communication, the ability to speak it fluently opens doors to countless opportunities. Whether you're a beginner eager to start your linguistic expedition or someone looking to enhance your existing skills, this workbook is your key to unlocking the power of spoken English.

Embark on a captivating journey that transcends traditional language learning methods. The pages ahead are filled with interactive exercises, practical tips, and engaging activities carefully curated to accelerate your English proficiency. Say goodbye to the fear of stumbling over words and hello to the confidence that comes with mastering a new language.

Are you ready to embark on this transformative voyage? Let's dive in, explore, and discover the joy of speaking English in no time!

Key Adjectives and Adverbs

Welcome to the exciting world of adjectives! In this section, we will delve into the power and versatility of adjectives, helping you add flair and detail to your English expressions.

Understanding Adjectives

Adjectives are words that describe or modify nouns. They provide more information about the characteristics, qualities, or attributes of a person, place, thing, or idea. Learning to use adjectives effectively will enhance your ability to express yourself clearly and vividly.

Types of Adjectives

Descriptive Adjectives: These adjectives paint a picture of the noun they modify. For example, in the phrase "a beautiful sunset," the word "beautiful" is a descriptive adjective.

Quantitative Adjectives: These adjectives indicate the quantity or amount of a noun. For instance, in the phrase "three apples," the word "three" is a quantitative adjective.

Demonstrative Adjectives: These adjectives point to a specific noun. Common demonstrative adjectives include "this," "that," "these," and "those." For instance, in the phrase "I love this book," the word "this" is a demonstrative adjective. Comparative and Superlative Adjectives: Adjectives can also express degrees of comparison. For example, "tall" can become "taller" (comparative) or "tallest" (superlative) when comparing the heights of different individuals.

Practical Tips for Using Adjectives

Be Specific: Instead of using generic adjectives, strive to be specific. Instead of saying "a big house," consider saying "a spacious mansion."

Placement Matters: Adjectives typically come before the noun they modify. For example, "a red car" or "an interesting book."

Avoid Redundancy: Be mindful of not overloading your descriptions with unnecessary adjectives. Choose words that add value and precision to your message.

Practice with Exercises: Engage in exercises that focus on adjectives. Create sentences, describe objects around you, and gradually incorporate adjectives into your daily vocabulary.

Exercises

Write five sentences describing your favorite place using descriptive adjectives.

Choose three objects in the room and create sentences using quantitative adjectives to describe their quantity.

Compare two of your favorite foods using comparative adjectives.

Express your preferences using demonstrative adjectives. For example, "I prefer this type of music."

By mastering adjectives, you'll elevate your language skills and make your communication more engaging. Enjoy the journey of exploring the vast world of adjectives in the English language!

Understanding Adverbs

Adverbs play a crucial role in enhancing the clarity and depth of your English communication. In this section, we'll delve into the fundamentals of adverbs, exploring their functions, types, and how to effectively use them to express a wide range of meanings.

Adverbs are versatile words that modify or describe verbs, adjectives, or other adverbs. They provide additional information about the manner, frequency, time, place, or degree of an action or quality. Understanding how to use adverbs appropriately is key to expressing yourself accurately and precisely in English.

Adverbs serve various functions, and recognizing these functions is essential for mastering their usage:

Modifying Verbs: Adverbs often describe how an action is performed. For example, in the sentence "She sang beautifully," the adverb "beautifully" modifies the verb "sang" by indicating the manner in which the singing occurred.

Modifying Adjectives: Adverbs can also enhance or limit the intensity of adjectives. In the phrase "a very tall building," the adverb "very" intensifies the adjective "tall."

Modifying Other Adverbs: Adverbs can modify other adverbs to provide additional details about the degree or manner. For instance, in the expression "He runs quite quickly," the adverb "quite" modifies the adverb "quickly."

Expressing Time, Place, and Frequency: Adverbs are essential for conveying temporal, spatial, and frequency-related information. Examples include "now," "here," and "often."

Types of Adverbs
Adverbs are categorized based on their functions. Common types include:

Adverbs of Manner: Describing how an action is performed, e.g., "slowly," "quickly."

Adverbs of Place: Indicating the location of an action, e.g., "here," "there."

Adverbs of Time: Providing information about when an action occurs, e.g., "now," "later."

Adverbs of Frequency: Describing how often an action takes place, e.g., "always," "rarely."

Placement of Adverbs
Understanding where to place adverbs within a sentence is crucial for maintaining clarity. In general, adverbs modify the word that directly follows them. However, there are exceptions and variations based on adverb types and sentence structures. Mastering adverbs will not only enhance your language skills but also contribute to the fluency and precision of your English expression.

Commonly Used Nouns

In English, nouns are the building blocks of communication. They represent people, places, things, or ideas. Mastering common nouns is crucial for effective communication. This section will introduce you to a variety of nouns that are frequently used in everyday conversations.

1. People Nouns:

Person: Refers to an individual.

Example: John is a friendly person.

Family: Represents members of a household.

Example: My family includes my parents, siblings, and grandparents.

2. Places Nouns:

City: Denotes a large urban area.

Example: New York City is known for its skyscrapers.

Restaurant: A place where people eat meals.

Example: Let's meet at the Italian restaurant for dinner.

3. Things Nouns:

Car: A vehicle for transportation.

Example: I drive a red car to work every day.

Book: An item for reading or studying.

Example: She enjoys reading novels and has a collection of books.

4. Ideas and Concepts Nouns:

Love: Represents a deep affection or strong attachment.

Example: Love is a powerful and positive emotion.

Freedom: The state of being free from constraints or oppression.

Example: Many people strive for freedom in their lives.

Remember to practice using these nouns in sentences to reinforce your understanding. Regular exposure and usage will enhance your English vocabulary and communication skills.

CHAPTER 32: Grammar Practice

Sentence Structure and Punctuation

In order to master English, it's essential to grasp the fundamental building blocks of communication – sentence structure. Sentences are the foundation of written and spoken language, and understanding how they are constructed will significantly enhance your ability to express ideas clearly.

1. Parts of a Sentence

A sentence is typically composed of two main parts: the subject and the predicate. The subject is the part of the sentence that tells us who or what the sentence is about. It is often a noun or pronoun. The predicate, on the other hand, contains the verb and provides information about the subject – what it is doing or what is happening.

Example: The cat (subject) is sleeping (predicate).

2. Types of Sentences

English sentences can be categorized into four main types: declarative, interrogative, imperative, and exclamatory.

Declarative sentences make statements or express opinions.

Example: She enjoys reading books.

Interrogative sentences ask questions.

Example: Have you finished your homework?

Imperative sentences give commands or make requests.

Example: Please pass the salt.

Exclamatory sentences convey strong emotions or excitement.

Example: What a beautiful sunset!

3. Sentence Construction

Understanding how to construct a sentence involves knowing the different elements that can be added to enhance its meaning. These include:

Modifiers: Words or phrases that provide additional information about the subject or the action in the sentence.

Example: The tall man (modifier) walked quickly (modifier) to catch the bus.

Objects: Nouns or pronouns that receive the action of the verb.

Example: She baked a delicious cake (cake is the object of the verb baked).

Complements: Words that complete the meaning of a sentence.

Example: The room smells (smells is completed by the complement bad).

4. Sentence Variety

Creating engaging and effective communication involves using a variety of sentence structures. Experiment with combining short and long sentences, varying your sentence beginnings, and incorporating different types of clauses. This diversity adds flair to your language and keeps your audience captivated.

Remember, the key to mastering sentence structure is practice. As you become more familiar with these components, you'll gain confidence in constructing sentences that convey your thoughts accurately and eloquently.

Understanding Sentence Punctuation

Punctuation plays a crucial role in conveying meaning and clarity in English sentences. Proper punctuation ensures that your writing is not only grammatically correct but also easily understandable. In this section, we'll explore the basics of sentence punctuation to help you navigate the intricacies of written English with confidence.

Period (.) - The Full Stop:

The period, also known as the full stop, is used to indicate the end of a declarative sentence. It brings closure to a thought and signals that a new sentence is about to begin.

Example:

I enjoy learning English. It opens up new opportunities for me.

Comma (,) - The Pause:

Commas are versatile punctuation marks used to indicate a pause or separate items in a list. They help clarify the structure of a sentence and make it easier to read.

Example:

Before we start our lesson, let's review the previous concepts.

I need to buy apples, oranges, and bananas from the grocery store.

Question Mark (?) - The Inquiry:

A question mark is used at the end of an interrogative sentence, signaling that the sentence is asking a question. Remember to adjust your intonation when reading a sentence ending in a question mark.

Example:

Have you completed your English homework?

What is your favorite aspect of learning a new language?

Exclamation Mark (!) - The Emphasis:

An exclamation mark is employed to express strong emotion, surprise, or emphasis. Use it sparingly to maintain its impact.

Example:

Wow! That was an amazing performance!

Be careful! The steps are slippery.

Colon (:) - The Introduction:

Colons are used to introduce a list, explanation, or quotation. They signal that what follows is directly related to the preceding clause.

Example:

There are three things you need to remember: practice, patience, and perseverance.

The teacher said it best: "Learning a new language is a journey, not a destination."

Semicolon (;) - The Link:

Semicolons are employed to connect two closely related independent clauses. They provide a stronger connection than a comma but not as strong as a period.

Example:

The rain stopped; the sun began to peek through the clouds.

She was busy with work; nonetheless, she made time for her language studies.

As you become more familiar with these punctuation marks, you'll gain confidence in constructing clear and effective sentences. Practice incorporating them into your writing to enhance your communication skills.

CHAPTER 33: Applying Verbs in Real-Life Scenarios

In this chapter, we will focus on practical and everyday English that you can use in your daily life. Mastering the art of daily conversations will not only help you communicate effectively but also build your confidence in using the English language. We will cover common daily routines and the corresponding conversations that often accompany them.

Daily Routines and Conversations

1. Morning Routine:
Example Conversation:
A: Good morning! How did you sleep?
B: Good morning! I slept well, thank you. How about you?
A: Not bad. I'm just getting ready for work. What's your plan for the day?

2. At Work:
Example Conversation:
A: Hi, how's your day going so far?
B: It's been busy. I have a meeting at 10 and a deadline to meet.
A: I understand. Let me know if you need any help.

3. Lunchtime:
Example Conversation:
A: Are you coming to lunch with us today?
B: I have a lot of work to finish, but I'll join you guys later.
A: Sure, we'll save you a seat.

4. Evening Routine:
Example Conversation:
A: How was your day?
B: It was long, but I'm glad it's over. How about yours?
A: Pretty good. I'm just going to relax and watch some TV.

5. Socializing:
Example Conversation:
A: We're having a small get-together this weekend. Are you interested?
B: That sounds fun! What time and where?
A: We're starting at 7 at my place. Can you make it?

Engaging in these daily conversations will not only help you improve your English but also make you feel more comfortable using it in various situations. Practice these dialogues regularly to enhance your language skills and feel more at ease in your English-speaking environment.

Planning and Discussing Future Events

In this section, we will focus on building your skills in planning and discussing future events in English. Being able to articulate your plans and engage in conversations about future happenings is a crucial aspect of effective communication. Let's explore some key phrases and structures to make this process easy and enjoyable.

1. Vocabulary for Future Events:

Before diving into conversations, let's enrich our vocabulary related to future events. Here are some essential terms:

Appointment: A prearranged meeting.

"I have a doctor's appointment next Tuesday."

Engagement: A planned social or professional meeting.

"Our engagement party is on Saturday."

Commitment: A promise or agreement to do something in the future.

"I have a work commitment on Thursday afternoon."

2. Verb Tenses for Future Events:

Mastering the correct verb tenses is vital for expressing future plans. Here are three common tenses:

Simple Future: Use it for actions that will happen at a specific time in the future.

"I will attend the conference next month."

Future Continuous: Describes an action that will be ongoing at a specific time in the future.

"This time tomorrow, I will be flying to Paris."

Future Perfect: Indicates an action that will be completed before a specific time in the future.

"By the end of the week, I will have finished my project."

3. Expressing Plans in Conversations:

Now, let's practice incorporating these tenses into conversations:

Making Plans:

"Would you like to grab coffee this weekend?"

"I'm planning to visit my family next month."

Confirming Plans:

"Sure, I'd love to meet for lunch on Friday."

"Yes, I'll definitely be at the party on Saturday."

Discussing Future Intentions:

"I'm thinking of taking a vacation in the summer."

"I hope to start a new course next year."

4. Interactive Exercises:

To reinforce your learning, engage in conversations with a language partner or use language learning apps that offer interactive exercises related to planning and discussing future events.

Remember, practice is key to improvement. The more you engage in conversations and express your future plans in English, the more confident and proficient you will become.

CHAPTER 34: Dialogue and Conversation Skills

Role-Playing Different Social Settings

Learning English isn't just about mastering grammar and vocabulary; it's also about being able to navigate various social situations confidently. Role-playing is a powerful tool that allows you to practice and enhance your language skills in different contexts. In this section, we'll explore how role-playing can be a fun and effective way for adult beginners to learn English while simulating real-life social scenarios.

1. Everyday Conversations:

Begin by simulating everyday conversations you might encounter, such as greetings, introducing yourself, and asking for directions. This helps you become comfortable with the basics and builds your confidence in casual interactions.

Example Scenario: Practice introducing yourself to a new neighbor or coworker.

2. Shopping Scenarios:

Role-playing shopping situations is an excellent way to learn essential vocabulary related to buying and selling. Focus on phrases like asking for assistance, negotiating prices, and expressing preferences.

Example Scenario: Simulate a conversation at a grocery store, asking for specific items and inquiring about promotions.

3. Restaurant Dialogues:

Practice ordering food, making reservations, and handling common restaurant interactions. This will not only improve your language skills but also prepare you for dining out in an English-speaking environment.

Example Scenario: Role-play ordering a meal at a restaurant, including dietary preferences and special requests.

4. Workplace Interactions:

For professional growth, simulate workplace conversations. This includes discussing projects, giving presentations, and engaging in small talk with colleagues. Example Scenario: Practice a brief presentation about your work or engage in a conversation during a coffee break.

5. Travel Situations:

Prepare for your next adventure by role-playing travel scenarios. This can include asking for directions, checking into a hotel, and interacting with fellow travelers.

Example Scenario: Simulate a conversation at an airport, including checking in, going through security, and asking for information.

6. Social Gatherings:

Enhance your social skills by role-playing conversations at parties or gatherings. This can help you feel more at ease in social settings, improving your ability to connect with others.

Example Scenario: Practice introducing yourself at a social event and engaging in small talk with new acquaintances.

Remember, the key to successful role-playing is to immerse yourself in each scenario and actively use the language. By incorporating these diverse social settings into your learning journey, you'll not only build your English proficiency but also gain the confidence to navigate a variety of real-life situations.

Understanding and Using Idioms

Learning idioms can be a fun and rewarding aspect of mastering the English language. Idioms are expressions that convey a figurative meaning, often different from the literal interpretation of the words used. Incorporating idioms into your language skills adds richness and nuance to your communication. Here's a guide on how to effectively use idioms in your English conversations:

Before using an idiom, ensure you understand its meaning. Idioms often have cultural or historical origins, so familiarize yourself with the context in which they are commonly used. Online resources, dictionaries, and context in real-life conversations can help you grasp their intended meanings.

Idioms work best when used in the right context. Consider the situation, topic, and the people you are communicating with. Using idioms that fit the context enhances your language skills and makes your communication more effective.

Begin by incorporating a few idioms into your conversations. Overloading your speech with idioms might be confusing for both you and your listener. Gradually introduce them to your vocabulary to build confidence and ensure proper usage.

Like any other aspect of language learning, practice is key. Try using idioms in everyday conversations, writing exercises, or even journaling. The more you use them, the more comfortable and natural they will become in your speech.

Listen to how native speakers use idioms in their conversations. This not only helps you understand the correct usage but also exposes you to the nuances of tone, intonation, and timing. Mimicking native speakers aids in improving your overall language proficiency.

Idioms often have cultural connotations, and their meanings can vary across regions. Be aware of these differences to avoid misunderstandings. If you're uncertain, it's perfectly acceptable to ask for clarification or guidance from native speakers.

Incorporate idioms into your writing to reinforce your understanding and usage. Whether in emails, essays, or creative writing, using idioms appropriately enhances the depth and expressiveness of your language.

Focus on learning commonly used idioms, as these are more likely to appear in everyday conversations. There are numerous resources, including books and websites, that provide lists of popular idioms along with their meanings and examples.

Remember, mastering idioms takes time and practice, so be patient with yourself. The more you immerse yourself in the language and actively use idioms, the more proficient you'll become. Enjoy the journey of incorporating these colorful expressions into your English communication!

Learning Common Idioms

Understanding idioms is a crucial aspect of mastering the English language. Idioms are expressions that convey a figurative meaning, often different from the literal interpretation of the words used. These phrases add color and depth to the language, making it more dynamic and rich. In this section, we will explore some common idioms that are frequently used in everyday English.

1. A Piece of Cake

Meaning: Extremely easy

Example: "Learning to use this new software is a piece of cake."

2. Hit the Hay

Meaning: Go to bed or go to sleep

Example: "I'm really tired; I think I'll hit the hay early tonight."

3. Break a Leg

Meaning: Good luck!

Example: "You're going to do great in your presentation – break a leg!"

4. Kick the Bucket

Meaning: To die

Example: "He's not sick anymore; unfortunately, he kicked the bucket yesterday."

5. Burn the Midnight Oil

Meaning: To work late into the night or early morning hours

Example: "I have a deadline tomorrow, so I'll be burning the midnight oil tonight."

6. Costs an Arm and a Leg

Meaning: Very expensive

Example: "Buying a new car can cost an arm and a leg."

As you encounter these idioms, take note of the context in which they are used. This will help you understand their meanings and use them appropriately in your own conversations. Incorporating idioms into your language skills adds a natural and native touch to your English proficiency.

To reinforce your learning, try using these idioms in sentences and conversations. This hands-on approach will not only solidify your understanding but also make your language skills more versatile and expressive.

CHAPTER 35: Reading and Comprehension

Reading and comprehension are fundamental skills that involve understanding and interpreting written information. Here are some ways to enhance your reading and comprehension skills:

Short Stories and News Articles

Reading short stories can be a highly effective and enjoyable way to enhance your English language skills. Short stories provide a concentrated dose of language in a compact form, making them ideal for adult beginners looking to improve their reading comprehension, vocabulary, and overall language proficiency. Here are some tips on how to make the most of your short story reading experience:

1. Choose Appropriate Stories:
Select short stories that match your current language proficiency level. Starting with stories that are too advanced may lead to frustration, while stories that are too easy might not provide sufficient challenge. Look for stories with a moderate level of difficulty to strike the right balance.

2. Read Actively:
Engage with the text actively by making predictions about the plot, characters, or outcomes. Stop periodically to reflect on what you've read, and ask yourself questions about the story. Active reading promotes better comprehension and retention of vocabulary.

3. Annotate and Highlight:
Don't be afraid to mark up the story. Highlight key phrases, new vocabulary, or sentences that you find interesting. Write notes in the margins to capture your thoughts and reactions. This helps reinforce your understanding and aids in future review.

4. Build Vocabulary:
Short stories are an excellent resource for expanding your vocabulary. Take note of unfamiliar words, look up their meanings, and try to use them in your own sentences. Consider maintaining a vocabulary journal to track and review new words regularly.

5. Discuss with Peers:
If possible, join a book club or language exchange group to discuss short stories with fellow learners. Sharing perspectives, opinions, and interpretations will not only deepen your understanding but also expose you to different ways of expressing ideas in English.

6. Set Realistic Goals:
Establish achievable reading goals, such as completing a certain number of short stories per week. Setting realistic targets will help you stay motivated and gradually improve your reading skills over time.

7. Explore Various Genres:

Diversify your reading experience by exploring short stories in different genres—science fiction, mystery, romance, and more. This exposure will broaden your vocabulary and help you adapt to various writing styles.

8. Reflect on Cultural Context:

Short stories often reflect cultural nuances and societal themes. Take a moment to consider the cultural context of the story, as this will deepen your understanding of language usage and idiomatic expressions.

9. Revisit and Review:

Periodically revisit the short stories you've read. Repetition enhances retention, and reviewing previously read material will solidify your grasp of vocabulary and grammar structures.

10. Enjoy the Process:

Finally, remember to enjoy the journey of learning through short stories. Find stories that captivate your interest and make the learning process an enjoyable and rewarding experience.

By incorporating these tips into your short story reading routine, you'll not only improve your English skills but also develop a lifelong love for literature in the English language.

Practice Reading the stories below following the tips outlined above:

Story 1: The Trip to Rome

A Country Mouse takes a trip to Rome to visit his cousin. At first, he is very confused by the big city and does not know how to act. For a few hours, he just sits quietly and watches what happens. He hears people say **Buongiorno** when they meet. He sees people order things quickly and keep to the right side of the street when walking. He also sees how quickly people walk. He sees that he must move quickly between their feet or they will step on him.

After he learns these things, he moves through the streets quickly and easily. He politely buys a piece of fruit from a mouse street vendor. He safely dodges through the crowds of people. Eventually, he reaches his cousin's house.

The cousin is happy to see him, but is surprised when he arrives in such good shape and with a piece of fruit as a gift as well. The Country Mouse explains that Rome is not so hard to get through if you do things in the Roman way.

Story 2: The Wise Old Owl

An old Owl lives for many years at the top of an oak tree. One day, a young Hawk happens by and asks him where he can find good hunting grounds. The Owl tells him about a place nearby where he can find what he is looking for. When this advice proves good, the Hawk tells his friends about it.

Next, a Bluebird comes by and asks the Owl about comfortable places to build a nest. The Owl tells her about an old barn nearby where she can find good shelter from the wind. Sure enough, the Bluebird finds that this advice is good.

As word gets around, more and more birds come to the Owl for advice. A pair of Swallows wait in line one early evening to ask the Owl some questions. The younger Swallow asks the older why everyone comes to the Owl for advice. The older Swallow explains that if one gives good advice there will be plenty of people who come to take it.

Story 3: The Patient Goat

A young Goat lives on a mountainside. He is often impatient and never wants to wait for anything. One day, he spots a lovely field nearby full of tall, green grass and fresh wheat. He wants to go into the field and eat, but a wooden fence is in the way. He tries to go over it. He tries to go around it. No matter what he does, he cannot find a way into the field.

He starts to bang his head into the fence. He tries to knock it down by force. The noise attracts the attention of a Gopher, who rushes over to see. The Gopher asks the Goat why he does this, and the Goat tells him he wants to get into the field. The Gopher explains that a farmer will come by in the afternoon and open a gate into the field. The Goat just has to wait.

Although he is not used to it, the Goat waits patiently near the gate. After a few hours, the farmer appears and opens the gate. Everything happens just as the Gopher says. The Goat enjoys the fine food in the field and spares his head from further damage.

How to Read News Articles

In the dynamic world of language acquisition, staying informed about current events is an excellent way to enhance your English proficiency. Reading news articles not only helps you expand your vocabulary but also exposes you to various grammatical structures and cultural nuances. Here are some effective strategies to navigate news articles as an adult beginner learning English:

Choose the Right Level:

Start with news articles that are specifically designed for beginners. Look for simplified versions or articles labeled as suitable for language learners. Gradually progress to more complex articles as your language skills improve.

Focus on Headlines:

Begin by reading the headlines. This practice helps you understand the main topic and sets the context for the article. Try to predict what the article might be about based on the headline.

Scan for Key Information:

Before delving into the details, scan the article to identify key information such as names, dates, and places. This preliminary step helps you grasp the basic facts before getting into the finer points.

Highlight Keywords:

While reading, highlight or underline keywords. This aids in recognizing important vocabulary and understanding the main ideas. You can then refer back to these keywords to reinforce your memory.

Break Down Sentences:

News articles often contain complex sentences. Break them down into smaller parts to understand the meaning more easily. Pay attention to sentence structures, and if needed, make use of dictionaries or language apps to look up unfamiliar words.

Utilize Visual Aids:

Many news articles include images, graphs, or charts. Use these visual aids to your advantage. They can provide additional context and help you comprehend the content more thoroughly.

Read Aloud:

Practice reading news articles aloud. This not only improves your pronunciation but also enhances your listening skills. Pay attention to the flow of the language and try to mimic the intonation and rhythm.

Discuss the News:

Engage in discussions about the news with native speakers or fellow learners. This not only reinforces your understanding of the articles but also helps you express your thoughts and opinions in English.

Diversify Sources:

Explore news articles from different sources to expose yourself to various writing styles and perspectives. This broadens your understanding of the language and allows you to adapt to different contexts.

Stay Consistent:

Regularly include news reading in your language learning routine. Consistency is key when it comes to language acquisition, and integrating news articles into your daily practice will contribute significantly to your progress.

By incorporating these strategies into your language learning journey, you can effectively use news articles as a valuable resource to enhance your English skills and stay well-informed about the world around you.

Understanding Context and Tone

Learning a new language involves more than just memorizing words and phrases; it requires an understanding of context and tone. Context and tone are like the dynamic duo of language comprehension, working hand in hand to convey meaning in a way that goes beyond literal translations. In this section, we'll delve into the significance of context and tone in English communication.

Context Matters

Imagine walking into a room where people are discussing a recent movie. Without context, it's challenging to grasp the essence of their conversation. Similarly, in language learning, context provides the backdrop against which words and sentences gain meaning. A single word can have different meanings depending on the context in which it is used.

Consider the word "bark." Without context, it could refer to the sound a dog makes or the protective outer covering of a tree. Understanding the context of a sentence helps you decipher which meaning is intended. As you progress in your English learning journey, pay attention to the surrounding words and situations to enhance your grasp of context.

The Nuances of Tone

Tone is the emotional quality that infuses language. It can convey feelings, attitudes, and intentions, influencing how a message is received. Mastering tone is essential for effective communication, as it allows you to express yourself with nuance and precision.

English, like any language, has a spectrum of tones – from formal to informal, polite to assertive. Consider the difference between saying "Could you please pass me the salt?" and "Hey, toss me the salt." The tone in each sentence varies, adapting to the formality of the situation.

To better understand tone, pay attention to the cultural and social context in which language is used. English speakers often adjust their tone based on factors like age, relationship, and the setting. By tuning into these nuances, you'll be better equipped to navigate diverse communication scenarios.

Developing a keen sense of context and tone takes practice. Engage in conversations, watch movies, and read a variety of texts to expose yourself to different contexts and tones. Observe how native speakers use language in various situations, and emulate their expressions.

CHAPTER 36: Writing Skills Development

Improving writing skills is a gradual process that involves practice, feedback, and a commitment to continuous learning. Here are some strategies to help you develop and enhance your writing skills:

Crafting Emails and Letters

Crafting effective emails and letters involves careful consideration of your audience, purpose, and tone. Whether you're writing a professional email, a formal letter, or a more casual message, the following tips can help you create clear, concise, and impactful communication:

General Tips:

Know Your Audience:

Tailor your language and tone to suit the recipient's expectations.

Consider the level of formality appropriate for the relationship.

Clear Purpose:

Clearly state the purpose of your email or letter in the opening lines.

Make it easy for the reader to understand the main message.

Conciseness:

Keep your message brief and to the point.

Avoid unnecessary details or information that might confuse the reader.

Professionalism:

Maintain a professional tone, even in casual communication.

Use proper grammar, punctuation, and spelling.

Subject Line:

Write a clear and concise subject line that summarizes the email's content.

This helps the recipient understand the importance of your message.

Email-Specific Tips:

Salutation:

Use an appropriate salutation based on your relationship with the recipient.

If unsure, a neutral greeting like "Dear [Name]" is usually safe.

Introduction:

Start with a friendly greeting.

Briefly introduce yourself if the recipient may not know you well.

Body:

Organize your thoughts into paragraphs for easy reading.

Use bullet points or numbered lists for clarity.

Keep paragraphs short for better readability.

Clarity and Structure:

Break down complex information into smaller sections.

Use headings or bold text to highlight important points.

Closing:

Summarize the main points in your closing remarks.

End with a clear call to action or a response prompt.

Signature:

Include a professional email signature with your contact information.

Letter-Specific Tips:

Formal Structure:

Follow a formal letter structure with a salutation, introduction, body, and closing.

Use appropriate letterhead if necessary.

Addressing the Recipient:

Be specific in addressing the recipient.

Use titles and last names unless you have a more casual relationship.

Closing:

End the letter with a formal closing (e.g., "Sincerely," "Best Regards," etc.).

Include your signature if it's a physical letter.

Address and Date:

Include the recipient's address and the date in the top-left corner.

Use a formal date format.

Subject:

Include a subject line for the recipient's reference.

Remember to proofread your emails and letters before sending to catch any errors or areas for improvement. Tailoring your communication to the specific context and audience will greatly enhance the effectiveness of your written correspondence.

Writing Descriptive Paragraphs

Descriptive writing is a powerful tool that allows you to paint vivid pictures with words. It helps the reader to visualize and connect with the subject, creating a more engaging reading experience. In this section, we will explore the key elements of writing effective descriptive paragraphs.

Use Detailed Language:

Incorporate sensory details such as sight, sound, touch, taste, and smell to bring your writing to life.

Choose specific adjectives and adverbs to convey precise meanings. Instead of saying "a big tree," consider "a towering oak with sprawling branches."

Create a Clear Image:

Clearly describe the subject of your paragraph so that readers can form a mental image. Provide enough detail to make it interesting without overwhelming the reader.

Organize Your Ideas:

Structure your descriptive paragraph logically. Start with a topic sentence that introduces the main idea, and then use supporting sentences to add details progressively.

Consider organizing details spatially, chronologically, or in order of importance to enhance coherence.

Appeal to Emotions:

Engage the reader emotionally by choosing words that evoke feelings. Describe not only how something looks but also how it makes you or others feel.

Show, Don't Tell:

Instead of simply stating facts, show them through descriptive language. For example, instead of saying "It was a beautiful sunset," describe the colors, the play of light, and the peaceful atmosphere.

Revise and Edit:

Take the time to review and refine your descriptive paragraphs. Ensure that each word serves a purpose and contributes to the overall image you want to convey.

Pay attention to grammar, punctuation, and sentence structure to enhance clarity.

Practice Writing Descriptive Paragraphs:

Sharpen your descriptive writing skills by practicing regularly. Choose various subjects to describe, from everyday objects to personal experiences, and experiment with different styles and tones.

Remember, the goal of descriptive writing is to transport your reader into the world you are describing. By mastering the art of descriptive paragraphs, you will not only improve your English language skills but also become a more compelling and effective communicator.

CHAPTER 37: English in Media and Entertainment

English plays a significant role in the media and entertainment industry, serving as the primary language for communication and expression in various forms of content. Here are some aspects of how English is utilized in media and entertainment:

Analyzing Song Lyrics and Movie Dialogues

Analyzing song lyrics and movie dialogues can provide insights into the themes, emotions, and cultural aspects of the work. Here are some common elements to consider when analyzing them:

Song Lyrics Analysis:
Lyricism:
Metaphors and Similes: Look for figurative language that adds depth and meaning to the lyrics.
Rhyme Scheme and Meter: Analyze the structure of the lyrics, including rhyme patterns and rhythm.
Theme and Message:
Central Theme: Identify the main theme or message of the song.
Narrative or Storytelling: Some songs tell a story or convey a sequence of events.
Emotional Tone:
Mood and Atmosphere: Determine the overall emotional tone of the lyrics.
Word Choice: Pay attention to the choice of words to convey specific emotions.
Cultural References:
Historical and Cultural Context: Consider any references to historical events, cultural phenomena, or societal issues.
Symbolism and Imagery:
Symbolic Elements: Identify symbols or recurring motifs that contribute to the meaning.
Visual Imagery: Look for vivid descriptions that create mental images.
Musical Elements:
Melody and Harmony: Consider how the musical composition complements or contrasts with the lyrics.
Instrumentation: Analyze the role of different instruments in conveying the song's emotions.
Movie Dialogues Analysis:
Characterization:
Speech Patterns: Examine how characters speak, including their tone, vocabulary, and style.
Consistency: Check for changes in dialogue style to reflect character development.

Plot Development:

Exposition: Identify how information about the plot, characters, or setting is revealed through dialogue.

Foreshadowing and Suspense: Look for instances where dialogue builds anticipation or hints at future events.

Conflict and Resolution:

Argumentation: Analyze dialogues during conflicts to understand character dynamics.

Resolution: Look for how dialogue contributes to the resolution of conflicts.

Cultural and Historical Context:

Slang and Dialect: Pay attention to language variations that reflect cultural or regional differences.

Historical References: Consider any references to historical events or cultural phenomena.

Humor and Wit:

Comic Relief: Identify instances of humor and wit, and analyze how they contribute to the overall tone.

Timing: Consider the timing and delivery of humorous lines.

Symbolism and Subtext:

Hidden Meanings: Look for dialogue that carries deeper meanings or subtext.

Symbolic Language: Identify symbols or metaphors used in dialogue.

Soundtrack and Sound Design:

Integration with Music: Examine how dialogue interacts with the film's soundtrack.

Silences: Consider the impact of pauses or moments of silence in dialogue.

Analyzing song lyrics and movie dialogues requires a combination of linguistic, literary, and cultural analysis to fully understand the artistic and thematic choices made by the creators.

Discussing TV Shows and Podcasts

TV shows and podcasts are popular forms of entertainment that have gained widespread popularity in recent years. They both offer unique ways to consume content and cater to different preferences and lifestyles.

TV Shows:

1. Narrative Excellence:

TV shows often provide a deep and immersive narrative experience. With multiple episodes in a season, creators have the opportunity to develop complex storylines and characters.

2. Visual Appeal:

The visual aspect of TV shows is a significant draw. High production values, special effects, and cinematography contribute to a visually stunning experience.

3. Genre Diversity:

TV shows cover a wide range of genres, from drama and comedy to science fiction and fantasy. This diversity allows viewers to find content that suits their tastes.

4. Cultural Impact:

Iconic TV shows can have a significant impact on popular culture. They create memorable characters, catchphrases, and moments that resonate with audiences worldwide.

5. Streaming Platforms:

The rise of streaming platforms has revolutionized TV consumption. Services like Netflix, Hulu, and Amazon Prime Video provide on-demand access to a vast library of shows, allowing viewers to binge-watch at their convenience.

Podcasts:

1. Accessibility:

Podcasts are highly accessible, with many available for free on various platforms. They offer a convenient way to consume content while commuting, exercising, or doing household chores.

2. Diverse Topics:

Podcasts cover an extensive range of topics, from true crime and history to science, technology, and personal development. This diversity allows listeners to explore their interests and discover new subjects.

3. Intimacy and Portability:

Podcasts often have an intimate and conversational feel. The medium allows hosts to connect with their audience, creating a sense of community. The portability of podcasts enhances this, as listeners can enjoy content wherever they go.

4. DIY Creativity:

Podcasting has a lower barrier to entry compared to traditional media. This has led to a surge in independent creators, fostering creativity and diverse voices.

5. Long-Form Content:

Podcasts often feature long-form discussions that allow for in-depth exploration of topics. This format suits those who prefer more extensive and nuanced conversations.

6. Learning and Education:

Many podcasts serve as educational tools, providing insights into various subjects. This makes them a valuable resource for continuous learning.

In summary, both TV shows and podcasts offer unique advantages, catering to different preferences and lifestyles. The rise of streaming platforms and the accessibility of podcasts have contributed to a golden age of content consumption, where audiences can enjoy a diverse array of entertainment on their terms.

CHAPTER 38: Cultural Insights and Language Usage

Cultural insights and language usage are closely intertwined, as language reflects and shapes the culture it is a part of. Here are some key aspects to consider:

Exploring English-Speaking Countries' Cultures

Exploring the cultures of English-speaking countries can be a fascinating journey, as each nation has its unique history, traditions, and customs. Here's a brief overview of the cultures of some major English-speaking countries:

United Kingdom (UK):

History: The UK has a rich history that includes medieval times, the Renaissance, and the Victorian era. Its monarchy, parliamentary system, and iconic landmarks such as Buckingham Palace and the Tower of London are integral to its cultural identity.

Literature: England is renowned for its literature, from William Shakespeare to Jane Austen and contemporary writers like J.K. Rowling.

Tea Culture: Tea is an essential part of British culture, with tea time being a cherished tradition.

United States (US):

Cultural Diversity: The U.S. is a melting pot of cultures due to its history of immigration. It has a diverse population, and each region may have its unique traditions.

Popular Culture: Hollywood, music, and literature play a significant role in shaping global pop culture. The U.S. is known for its influence on entertainment worldwide.

Thanksgiving: A significant holiday, celebrated with a traditional feast, symbolizing gratitude and togetherness.

Canada:

Multiculturalism: Canada prides itself on being a multicultural society, with influences from Indigenous peoples, French and British colonists, and a diverse immigrant population.

Nature and Outdoor Activities: Canadians often engage in outdoor activities like hiking, skiing, and ice hockey, reflecting the country's vast natural landscapes.

Bilingualism: Canada is officially bilingual, with English and French as official languages.

Australia:

Outdoor Lifestyle: Australians have a strong connection to outdoor activities like surfing, barbecues, and sports due to the country's climate and geography.

Aboriginal Culture: Indigenous Australian cultures are integral to the nation's identity, with a rich history of art, Dreamtime stories, and traditions.

Laid-Back Attitude: The Australian culture is often characterized by a laid-back and friendly attitude.

New Zealand:
Māori Influence: Māori culture is an essential part of New Zealand's identity, with traditions like the haka, and Māori language being officially recognized.
Adventure Sports: New Zealand is known for its outdoor adventure sports like bungee jumping, skydiving, and hiking in stunning landscapes.
Film Industry: The country gained international recognition through the film industry, especially with the "Lord of the Rings" trilogy.
While these are broad generalizations, it's crucial to note that each country contains a diverse range of subcultures, and there can be variations within regions. Exploring these cultures through travel, literature, and conversations can provide a deeper understanding of the rich tapestry of English-speaking societies.

Understanding Regional Variations in English

English is a highly diverse language with numerous regional variations, often influenced by historical, cultural, and geographical factors. These variations manifest in differences in pronunciation, vocabulary, grammar, and even idiomatic expressions. The main regional variations include:

British English (UK English):
Received Pronunciation (RP) is often considered the standard accent, but there is significant regional variation in accents such as Cockney, Estuary English, Scottish English, Welsh English, and more.
Vocabulary differences: Some words have different meanings or are unique to British English (e.g., "lorry" for truck, "boot" for trunk, "biscuit" for cookie).
American English:
Pronunciation differences: American English has various accents, such as General American, Southern, Midwestern, and more. Pronunciation of certain vowels and consonants can differ significantly.
Vocabulary differences: Some words have different meanings or are specific to American English (e.g., "truck" for lorry, "trunk" for boot, "cookie" for biscuit).
Canadian English:
Similar to American English in many respects but with some distinct features, including certain spelling preferences (e.g., "colour" instead of "color") and regional accents.
Australian English:
Pronunciation differences: Australian English has unique vowel sounds, and there are regional accents such as the broad Australian accent.
Vocabulary differences: Some words are unique to Australian English or have different meanings (e.g., "ute" for pickup truck, "thongs" for flip-flops).

New Zealand English:
Similar to Australian English in many aspects but with some differences in pronunciation and vocabulary.

South African English:
Influenced by Dutch, Malay, and indigenous languages, South African English has unique features in pronunciation and vocabulary.

Indian English:
Diverse due to India's multilingual and multicultural context. Pronunciation, vocabulary, and grammar may vary across regions.

Caribbean English:
Influenced by various languages, including African languages, Caribbean English has unique accents, vocabulary, and expressions.

Singaporean English:
Reflects the multicultural nature of Singapore, with influences from English, Chinese, Malay, and Tamil. Vocabulary and pronunciation can vary.

Nigerian English:
Reflects the linguistic diversity of Nigeria, with influences from indigenous languages. Pronunciation and vocabulary may vary across regions.

Understanding regional variations in English is crucial for effective communication, as speakers may encounter differences in pronunciation, vocabulary, and expressions when interacting with people from different parts of the world. Language continues to evolve, and regional variations contribute to its richness and diversity.

CHAPTER 39: Comprehensive Final Assessment

Testing Grammar Exercise

Question 1:
Identify the subject and predicate in the following sentence:
"The cat sat on the windowsill."
Answer 1:
Subject: The cat
Predicate: sat on the windowsill

Question 2:
Choose the correct form of the verb in the following sentence:
"She _____ to the store every day."
a) go   b) goes   c) going
Answer 2:
b) goes

Question 3:
Correct the following sentence:
"He don't like pizza."
Answer 3:
"He doesn't like pizza."

Question 4:
Identify the type of sentence:
"Are you coming to the party?"
Answer 4:
Interrogative sentence

Question 5:
Choose the correct word to complete the sentence:
*"I have _____ interesting book to read."
a) an   b) a   c) the
Answer 5:
a) an

Question 6:
Identify the conjunction in the following sentence:
"She likes both chocolate and vanilla ice cream."
Answer 6:
and

Question 7:
Select the correct pronoun for the blank:
"Someone left _____ umbrella in the hallway."
a) their   b) his   c) its
Answer 7:
a) their

Question 8:
Correct the punctuation in the following sentence:
"I can't believe she said "that" to me."
Answer 8:
"I can't believe she said 'that' to me."

Question 9:
Choose the correct preposition to complete the sentence:
"She is allergic _____ cats."
a) to   b) with   c) for
Answer 9:
a) to

Question 10:
Identify the tense of the verb in the following sentence:
"They will finish the project by tomorrow."
Answer 10:
Future tense

Vocabulary, and Comprehension Exercises

Question: What does the word "ubiquitous" mean?
Answer: "Ubiquitous" means present, appearing, or found everywhere.
Word: Meticulous

Question: Provide a synonym for the word "meticulous."
Answer: A synonym for "meticulous" is "thorough" or "precise."
Word: Pernicious

Question: Can you give an example of something that could be described as "pernicious"?
Answer: An example of something "pernicious" might be a harmful influence or a destructive habit.
Word: Ambivalent

Question: Describe a situation in which someone might feel ambivalent.
Answer: Someone might feel ambivalent when faced with a difficult decision where there are both positive and negative aspects.
Word: Serendipity

Question: Explain the meaning of the term "serendipity."
Answer: "Serendipity" refers to the occurrence and development of events by chance in a happy or beneficial way.

Comprehension Questions:
Passage: In a story, the protagonist faces a moral dilemma. How does this challenge contribute to the development of the plot?

Question: How does the protagonist's moral dilemma contribute to the plot's development?
Answer: The protagonist's moral dilemma adds complexity and tension to the plot, forcing them to make challenging decisions that shape the story's direction.
Passage: The setting of the narrative is a small coastal town. How does the environment impact the characters' experiences and interactions?

Question: In what ways does the coastal town setting impact the characters' experiences and interactions?
Answer: The coastal town setting can influence the characters' lifestyles, relationships, and daily challenges, providing a backdrop that shapes their actions and decisions.
Passage: The author employs vivid imagery to describe the scene. How does the use of imagery enhance the reader's understanding of the story?

Question: How does the use of vivid imagery enhance the reader's understanding of the story?
Answer: Vivid imagery helps create a mental picture for the reader, making the story more immersive and allowing them to better connect with the narrative.
Passage: The story employs flashbacks to reveal the character's past. How does this narrative technique contribute to the overall storytelling?

Question: How does the use of flashbacks contribute to the overall storytelling?
Answer: Flashbacks provide insight into the character's past, adding depth and context to their present actions and motivations.
Passage: The narrative employs symbolism to represent the theme of freedom. Can you identify a specific symbol and explain its significance?

Question: Identify a symbol in the narrative that represents the theme of freedom and explain its significance.

Answer: One symbol representing freedom in the narrative is [specific symbol]. Its significance lies in [explanation of its role in conveying the theme of freedom].

Oral and Written Communication Skills Exercise

Improving both oral and written communication skills is crucial for effective communication in various personal and professional settings. Here are some exercises that can help enhance these skills:

Oral Communication Skills Exercises:
Public Speaking:
Choose a topic and practice giving a short speech in front of a mirror.
Present your ideas to a small group of friends or family.
Join a public speaking club like Toastmasters to receive constructive feedback.

Role-playing:
Engage in role-playing scenarios to simulate real-life conversations.
Practice negotiating, handling conflicts, or giving feedback in different scenarios.

Storytelling:
Share personal anecdotes or experiences with friends to enhance storytelling abilities.
Work on structuring stories with a clear beginning, middle, and end.

Debates:
Participate in debates on topics of interest to improve your ability to think on your feet.
Practice defending both sides of an argument to enhance critical thinking.

Telephone Skills:
Conduct phone conversations to improve clarity and tone.
Practice leaving voicemails with concise and relevant information.

Interview Practice:
Simulate job interviews with a friend or family member.
Focus on articulating your strengths, experiences, and career goals clearly.

Active Listening:
Engage in active listening exercises where you repeat or summarize what someone has said.
Practice maintaining eye contact and avoiding distractions during conversations.

Written Communication Skills Exercises:
Journaling:
Start a personal or professional journal to practice expressing thoughts in writing.
Set aside time each day to write about your experiences or reflect on your goals.

Editing Practice:

Take a written piece and edit it for clarity, grammar, and conciseness.

Ask someone else to review your writing and provide constructive feedback.

Email Correspondence:

Practice writing clear and concise emails.

Pay attention to formatting, tone, and appropriate language.

Essay Writing:

Select a topic and write an essay with a clear introduction, body, and conclusion.

Focus on organizing ideas logically and supporting arguments effectively.

Creative Writing:

Experiment with different writing styles through short stories, poems, or fictional pieces.

Explore descriptive language and creative expression.

Professional Documents:

Draft and refine resumes, cover letters, and LinkedIn profiles.

Ensure that these documents effectively showcase your skills and experiences.

Peer Review:

Exchange written work with peers for feedback.

Provide constructive criticism and actively implement suggestions.

Remember to consistently practice these exercises to see gradual improvement in both oral and written communication skills. Additionally, seeking feedback from others and being open to constructive criticism is crucial for continuous growth.

Additional Exercises

Exercise 1:

Fill in the blanks with the words from the boxes. One extra word will not be used. Then, if possible, practice the dialogue with a partner.

are	is	leaves	do	is
doesn't	do	are	understand	think
does	have	works	is	don't

A: Excuse me, _____ you Helen?

B: Yes, I am. _____ I know you?

A: No, but you _____ in my English class.

B: Oh, what's your name?

A: My name _____ Adriana. And you?

B: My name is Brian. What do you _____ about our teacher?

A: She _____ know how to teach. She_____ always late. I don't _____ her.

B: Yeah, she _____ class early too.

A: _____ you want to do the homework together? I _____ understand it.

B: Yeah, let's do it. Do you _____ time now?

A: No, I have to go now, but maybe later this afternoon.

B: _____ 3:00 work for you?

A: Yes, that _____ for me. I'll see you then.

B: Ok, see you.

Answers

A: Excuse me, ...*are*... you Helen?

B: Yes, I am. ....*Do*.... I know you?

A: No, but you .....*are*.... in my English class.

B: Oh, what's your name?

A: My name ....*is*....... Adriana. And you?

B: My name is Brian. What do you ......*think*..... about our teacher?

A: She ....*doesn't*...... know how to teach. She ....*is*....always late. I don't ...*understand*...her.

B: Yeah, she ......*leaves*..... class early too.

A: .....*Do*....... you want to do the homework together? I ......*don't*...... understand it.

B: Yeah, let's do it. Do you ....*have*...... time now?

A: No, I have to go now, but maybe later this afternoon.

B: ....*Does*..... 3:00 work for you?

A: Yes, that ......*works*..... for me. I'll see you then.

B: Ok, see you.

Exercise 3:

They doesn't want more food.

Do you married?

Are you eat pizza?

She live at home with her parents.

The computer is not work very well.

Answers

They doesn't want *more food. They don't want* more food. / She doesn't want more food.

Do *you married? Are* you married?

Are you eat *pizza? Do* you eat pizza?

She **live** *at home with her parents.* She *lives* at home with her parents.

The computer **is** *not work very well.* The computer *does* not work very well.

Exercise 4:

Fill in the blanks with the correct form of the verb in the Past Simple. For a more complete list of irregular verbs, see Appendix A.

Verb	Past Simple Form
take	
have	
get	
see	
make	
eat	
write	
think	
come	
leave	
go	
drive	
find	
buy	
fall	
know	
give	
break	
feel	
meet	
do	
read	
say	
tell	
understand	

Answers

Verb	Past Simple Form
take	took
have	had
get	got
see	saw
make	made
eat	ate

write	wrote
think	thought
come	came
leave	left
go	went
drive	drove
find	found
buy	bought
fall	fell
know	knew
give	gave
break	broke
feel	felt
meet	met
do	did
read	read
say	said
tell	told
understand	understood

Exercise 5:

Each sentence has a mistake. Identify the error and correct the sentence.

Who you saw last night at the party?

I leaved the house at 8:00 this morning.

Do you get the book yesterday?

Was you at the bank this morning?

I called you last night, but you didn't answered.

Why you were not at work today?

I was not eat because I was not hungry.

Answers

- **Who** did you see **last night at the party?**
- **I** left **the house at 8:00 this morning.**
- Did **you get the book yesterday?**
- Were you **at the bank this morning?**
- **I called you last night, but you** didn't answer.
- **Why** were you **not at work today?**
- **I** didn't eat **because I was not hungry.**

Exercise 6

Fill in the blank with the Past Simple form of the verb in parentheses. Some verbs may be irregular, and some ask for the negative form.

Yesterday Sara _____ to the concert. (go)

Last week I _____ her at the mall. (see)

My cousins _____ at the meeting. (be)

You _____ extra clothes. I have enough here. (not need)

My brothers and I _____ home. (not be)

Mike _____ for two hours yesterday. (surf)

Last year I _____ in school. Now I'm working. (be)

We _____ that you were in the hospital. (not know)

My computer _____ working this morning. (stop)

The students _____ class early. (leave)

Directions: Use the words below to make questions in the Past Simple tense.

- (Where/ you/ be/ yesterday)
- (you/ have fun/ yesterday)
- (I/ late/ be/ last week)
- (he/ eat dinner)
- (they/ be/ at the movies with you)
- (When / they/ come home)
- (What/ the answer/ be)
- (Why/ you/ do that)
- (Who/ you with/ be)
- (How/ get here/ she)

Answers

Yesterday Sara **......went.....** to the concert. (go)

Last week I **.............saw.......** her at the mall. (see)

My cousins **..........were.........** at the meeting. (be)

You **...........didn't need......** extra clothes. I have enough here. (not need)

My brothers and I **..........were not..........** home. (not be)

Mike **..........surfed..........** for two hours yesterday. (surf)

Last year I **............was...........** in school. Now I'm working. (be)

We **.................didn't know.........** that you were in the hospital. (not know)

My computer **..............stopped......** working this morning. (stop)

The students **..............left..........** class early. (leave)

(Where/ you/ be/ yesterday) **Where were you yesterday?**

(you/ have fun/ yesterday) Did you have fun yesterday?

(I/ late/ be/ last week) **Was I late last week?**

(he/ eat dinner) Did he eat dinner?

(they/ be/ at the movies with you) **Were they at the movies with you?**

(When / they/ come home) **When did they come home?**

(What/ the answer/ be) **What was the answer?**

(Why/ you/ do that) Why did you do that?
(Who/ you with/ be) **Who were you with?**
(How/ get here/ she) **How did she get here?**

CHAPTER 40: Useful Language Resources and Tools

Here are 10 useful English language resources and tools:

Grammarly: A powerful writing assistant that helps you check grammar, spelling, and punctuation errors. It also provides suggestions for improving your writing style.

Merriam-Webster Online Dictionary: A reliable online dictionary that provides definitions, synonyms, and pronunciation of words.

Thesaurus.com: A comprehensive online thesaurus that helps you find synonyms and antonyms for words, enhancing your vocabulary.

Google Translate: While not perfect, Google Translate can be a helpful tool for quick translations and understanding phrases in different languages.

Cambridge Dictionary: Another reputable online dictionary with clear definitions, examples, and audio pronunciations.

WordReference: A valuable online resource for translations, language forums, and language-related discussions.

Readable: This tool analyzes the readability of your text, helping you make it more accessible to your target audience.

BBC Learning English: A platform offering a variety of resources to improve English language skills, including videos, audio, and interactive lessons.

Purdue OWL (Online Writing Lab): A comprehensive writing resource from Purdue University that provides guidelines on grammar, writing style, and citation formats.

Vocabulary.com: An interactive platform that helps you improve your vocabulary through engaging games, quizzes, and challenges.

These resources can be beneficial for learners, writers, and anyone looking to enhance their English language skills.

CHAPTER 41: Next Steps in English Mastery

Mastering English involves a combination of consistent practice, exposure, and a focused approach to learning. Here are 10 tips to help you enhance your English **language skills:**

Read Regularly:

Read a variety of materials, including books, articles, newspapers, and blogs. This exposure to different styles of writing will improve your vocabulary and comprehension.

Expand Your Vocabulary:

Learn new words every day and try to use them in your conversations and writing. Use flashcards or vocabulary apps to reinforce your learning.

Practice Listening:

Listen to English podcasts, audiobooks, and news broadcasts. This will help you understand different accents, improve your listening skills, and expose you to various expressions and idioms.

Speak Aloud:

Practice speaking English every day. This can be done by talking to yourself, participating in language exchange programs, or finding a language partner. Speaking aloud helps improve pronunciation and fluency.

Write Regularly:

Write something every day. You can write in your diary, keep a journal, start a blog, or just use English more in your daily communication. The more you do it, the more you'll see your confidence and skills improving. This is your final assignment. Keep working at it, keep learning, and remember, your last mistake is your best teacher. Keep a journal, write essays, or start a blog. Regular writing helps improve grammar, sentence structure, and overall communication skills. Seek feedback to identify areas for improvement.

Grammar and Punctuation:

Pay attention to grammar rules and punctuation. Understanding the basics of English grammar will make your communication more precise and effective.

Use Technology:

Utilize language learning apps, online courses, and language exchange platforms. Many apps offer interactive exercises and games to make learning enjoyable.

Immerse Yourself:

Surround yourself with English as much as possible. Change the language settings on your devices, watch movies and TV shows in English, and engage with English-speaking communities online.

Join Language Classes:

Enroll in English language courses or workshops. Formal education can provide structured learning and opportunities for interaction with teachers and peers.

Stay Consistent:

Language mastery takes time and consistent effort. Set realistic goals, create a study routine, and stay committed to your learning journey.

Remember, the key to mastering any language is consistent practice and exposure. Be patient with yourself, celebrate small victories, and enjoy the process of learning.

Conclusion

In conclusion, as we journeyed through the pages of "THE EASY WAY TO LEARN ENGLISH FOR ADULT BEGINNERS," one question reverberates: Have you discovered the power within yourself to embrace the English language with confidence and ease? Learning a new language can be a daunting task, particularly for adult beginners. Yet, within these chapters, we've explored not just the intricacies of English grammar and vocabulary but also the resilience and potential that reside within each learner. The question posed is not merely rhetorical; it serves as a reflection on the transformative journey you've undertaken.

With every lesson, exercise, and anecdote, we aimed to demystify the complexities of English, offering a pathway that is accessible, engaging, and, dare we say, enjoyable. The process of language acquisition is not just about mastering syntax and semantics; it is about finding joy in communication, expressing oneself with newfound fluency, and breaking down the barriers that language may present.
As you close this book, consider how far you've come. Have you conquered the challenges that once seemed insurmountable? Do you now approach English not as an intimidating puzzle, but as a tool that empowers you to connect, understand, and articulate your thoughts?

The journey to English proficiency is ongoing, but armed with the knowledge and skills imparted within these pages, you are better equipped to face the linguistic landscape ahead. Embrace the language with curiosity, make mistakes without fear, and relish the moments when you find yourself effortlessly conversing in English.
Remember, the easy way to learn English is not about shortcuts or quick fixes; it's about embracing the process, enjoying the discoveries, and celebrating the victories, no matter how small. So, as you step into the world armed with a newfound linguistic prowess, ask yourself again: Have you unlocked the easy way to learn English for yourself? The answer lies within your journey, a testament to your dedication, persistence, and the belief that learning, at any age, is a rewarding adventure.
Good luck!!!

EXTRA BONUS

Scan the QRCODE and download your BONUS EXTRA which includes FLASHCARDS + PICTURE DICTIONARY + WORD MATCH + DICTIONARY:

Made in United States
Troutdale, OR
11/30/2024